Locking the Cookie Jar ™
(How to Protect Against Embezzlement, Identity Theft, and Hackers)
by **R. Scott Alvord**, MBA-MCA, BSCS

1. Nonfiction > Computers > Security > Online Safety & Privacy.
2. Nonfiction > Business & Economics > Money & Monetary Policy

ISBN-13: 978-1-942836-50-6

Editing by Kyler Alvord
Cover design by Jerry Jozwiak
Book layout by Keither Alvord

The text of this book is set in Cambria font

Printed in the United States of America

Advanced Publishing Concepts
(a division of Advanced Development Concepts, LLC)
141 Bogart Ct., Roseville, CA 95747 (916) 782-4272
www.AdvancedPublishingConcepts.com

Locking the Cookie Jar ™

How to Protect Against Embezzlement, Identity Theft, and Hackers

By:

R. Scott Alvord, MBA-MCA, BSCS

Dedication

Raymond C. Alvord (7/7/1942 – 3/20/2017). My father. Retired from the military, a cop, animal lover, and an auto mechanic that kept our neighbors' cars in shape. When he was a police officer, I used to do ride-alongs with him where I saw how heartless people could be toward each other's property and safety.

I flew to New York and said my final goodbye to him in January, while finishing up this book. The final hug tore me up inside because we both knew it would be the last. Shortly after I left, he discovered that the years of emphysema was not the only thing killing him. He had stage 4 cancer in many major organs and it killed him quickly. A week after his death, I found a voicemail on my cell phone from two weeks earlier. He assured me that we were good with our relationship and that he loved me. Perfect encore. He would have bragged about this book.

Acknowledgments

This section is where I'm supposed to list all the zillions of people who helped make this book a reality including the doctor who delivered me, my teachers who blah blah blah. However, after thinking about it for a while, I decided that because I have other books either completed or in the works that have extensive acknowledgments, I'd like to list those who REALLY influenced and helped *this* particular book.

David Stuart. David is my best buddy from college, a best man at my wedding, and probably the smartest person I know. David is a professor at UC Santa Barbara, and although he'd never admit it, he's also one of the world's top particle physicists. If I was a contestant on the TV game show *Who Wants to be a Millionaire?*, David would be the first person I'd call if I had to use a lifeline. He not only helped me understand my calculus classes, but he was my chess opponent and encryption challenger throughout college. It was this last part, the encryption part, that was the most relevant for this book. David and I used to encrypt messages back and forth to each other and challenge each other to figure out how to decrypt them. I started to appreciate the challenge, which led me to develop an extensive encryption algorithm that I still feel is excellent. Scientific creativity is what a lot of our conversations can be summarized as and I appreciate that about him.

Larry Roth. Larry was one of my computer science professors in college. I found him to be the most practical of my professors because he figured out how to work real-life situations into the assignments instead of just theory. My senior project mentioned in this book was for his class. How he handled my "hacking of the student body passwords" was encouraging. Yes, I fell asleep during a Digital Logic final exam in his class, but it certainly wasn't a reflection of his teaching.

Kyler Alvord. Our youngest of seven children. Kyler discovered his love for writing during his sophomore year of college at Walla Walla University where he's a communications major. As parents, we knew it was his gift but it took him a year to realize it himself. During the writing of this book, he was an editor and journalist for College Magazine and a writer for his college's newspaper. He will have finished interning for CBS This Morning in New York City as this book goes to print. Because I know he's very detail-oriented and highly skilled, I asked him if he'd be the editor for this book and he agreed. If you find any typos, it's probably because I changed something after he edited it. I love you son.

Keither Alvord. My middle son. Keither was undergoing significant changes in his life as I started this book. Not only did he graduate with a business/marketing degree from Sacramento State University, but he started a job with a client and long-time family friend. Oh yeah, and he got married a few weeks after graduating and moved into a new home with his bride. Keither is an expert at InDesign, the primary tool used to professionally format books. My company has used his skills previously, so naturally he's the first choice for this one. Thank you Keither. I love you son.

Finally, to my **Lord and Savior, Jesus Christ**, the *Footprints in the Sand* poem describes my life. I have had some incredibly difficult times, times that almost ended my life. Yet He carried me through them. I have witnessed absolute miracles and I have been blessed in many ways that I do not deserve, but for which I will take the responsibility to use those gifts to help others. I see His hand and feel His presence and while I am far from where I need to be in my walk with Him, I strive to use my talents to share His love and further His work. I thank my Savior for loving me unconditionally.

Author's Foreword

The Delay

A few clients and friends knew this book was coming and we thought it would be in the fall of 2016. I had it essentially completed this book more than a year ago but then I decided to run as a candidate for a local office (city council). The campaign took a whole year and because it was one of the largest ground games this city has seen in decades, I was very busy and gave up on writing altogether. The Thursday before Election Tuesday in November, I flew to Thousand Oaks, California, in the evening, checked into a hotel for the night, presented a two-hour seminar called *How to Hacker-proof your Business and Life* at the PICA Conference (for Private Investigators) on Friday, then raced to the airport to fly back home. This conference forced me to finish the final section of the book and also prompted me to add in a "small" piece that came to mind while answering questions at the conference. Looking back, I believe the campaign delay was perfect because I was not in a position to properly finish or publish the book. Now I am.

How did the campaign turn out? It was sweet. I got elected! It was another example of how hard work will eventually pay off. Ramping up on city policies and regional politics took four months.

What's Missing

This book could be a LOT thicker. I could write sections on various hardware and network configuration schemes that stop hackers. However, this technology changes all the time and that kind of detail will be limited to a narrow, high-tech audience. I plan to create an online resource for various hardware and software solutions and it will allow me to change them as time passes. If I write about some of them in this book, the book will be quickly outdated.

I also took out extra fluff and decided to write towards the real weak link in any home or business: the individual user. It's the individual person, employee, or manager that often enables embezzlement or hacking. Their ignorance of how it's done causes them to let their guard down. This is when they become prey to the unethical legion of hawks gliding above us, waiting for a mistake. I decided to first explain how it's done. Then when we talk about solutions, they make a lot more sense and are taken more seriously.

I share a lot of stories and examples of security failures. Often these are real stories that have sometimes been slightly modified to protect the identity of the victims or criminals. In a few cases, I added a story that is really a fictional simplification of multiple real stories just like it.

Was I or Was I Not?

I often get asked if I was a hacker who broke into computer systems or an embezzler speaking from experience. I understand that if I was a master criminal speaking from experience, it might make the book more legitimate even though the author might be a retired scumbag.

I was never an embezzler in the way that most might think. I've never embezzled from the outside. When I stole from a company, it was as an ignorant employee. To be completely transparent, I was like most employees. In fact, I think I was like all employees at some time in their career, if they were truthful. The only type of embezzling I ever did was through time and materials. It was never significant but as a younger employee, I'm sure I did plenty of personal things on company time including talking about the playoffs, printing personal things on company printers using company paper and ink, and I took home my share of company pens that probably never made their way back to work. These are all forms of embezzlement and while they are very common, they are still wrong without company permission. I honestly believe I was more ignorant than purposeful when it came to stealing time, paper, or pens. When I became an employer, I was quick to clarify what was allowable and what required permission while at work. I didn't care about occasional personal conversations, a few pens going home, or occasionally checking text messages while at work; but I did care about many other things.

www.LockingTheCookieJar.com

I never viewed myself as a hacker, but as I look back, I suppose I was. I was not the type of hacker that you read about in the news. I did some impressive hacking as a younger programmer and I broke several encryption schemes in the process. I wanted to see what I was capable of doing, but never opened confidential files or did any damage to digital information. I enjoyed the challenge of figuring out how to hack an account or a file more than I wanted to see what was behind the account or inside the file. It was the equivalent of picking a lock and opening the door, but never going inside. I was different than the hackers I knew about because they always bragged about what they did and sometimes even shared the details to prove it. Other than my senior project (described in this book), I never shared what I did or how I did it. Although it was still wrong, I can look myself in the mirror and feel comfortable that I never ever did any damage or risked the security of any individual or company.

As I grew older, I decided that the risk and embarrassment of getting caught was not worth the challenge. I have used my skills to do a few "white hat" hacking projects, but never ever for unethical purposes. Technology is changing so rapidly that I don't have the time to be a skilled or successful hacker even if I wanted to be.

Free Gift!
The embezzlement part of this book is based on chapters from an upcoming book, *Fire Your Job, Hire Yourself*. If you are entrepreneurial in nature, you'll love some quality material taken directly from that book. Follow this link to get a free eBook and/or other gifts we'll provide over time:

https://LockingTheCookieJar.com/giftbk

Shameless Plug:
If you like this book AND own a business or have business clients, you will LOVE our Locking the Cookie Jar Seminar! You can find out more at:

https://LockingTheCookieJar.com/seminarbk

Table of Contents

Chapter and Section	Page
Dedication	**5**
Acknowledgments	**7**
Author's Forward	**9**
Table of Contents	**13**
Locking the Cookie Jar (Introduction)	**19**

1) **Embezzlement Schemes** (non-business owners can skip) — **21**
This section explains the specific techniques that your internal employees and others can use to steal from you, and how to stop them. Understanding their strategy is the foundation for protecting yourself.

• Cash Embezzlement Schemes	23
a) Most Common Forms of Cash Embezzlement	23
b) Best Techniques to Help Protect Against Cash Embezzlement	23
• Negotiable Document Embezzlement Schemes	27
a) Most Common Forms of Negotiable Document Embezzlement	27
b) Best Techniques to Help Protect Against Negotiable Document Embezzlement	27
• Account Credit Embezzlement Schemes	29
a) Most Common Forms of Credit Embezzlement	29
b) Best Techniques to Help Protect Against Credit Embezzlement	30
• Physical Item Embezzlement Schemes	33
a) Most Common Forms of Item Embezzlement	33

b) Best Techniques to Help Protect Against Item Embezzlement   33

- Computer-based Embezzlement Schemes   35
  a) Most Common Forms of Computer-based Embezzlement   35
  b) Best Techniques to Help Protect Against Computer-based Embezzlement   36
- Summary of Effective Deterrents to Embezzlement   39

2) **Hacking the Hacker's Mind**   45

This section is important! Hackers can be dangerous to both people and companies. Learn how they can hack into your accounts, what motivates them, and how to avoid being an easy target.

- Hacker by Definition   45
- The Majority of Bottom Feeders   47
  a) Trojan Horses Start as Innocent Ponies   47
  b) Phishing for Phools   47
- What Kind of Damage Can a Hacker Impose?   53
  a) Case Study #1, Goodbye Retirement   53
  b) Case Study #2, Healthcare Confidentiality...NOT   53
  c) Case Study #3, Disgruntled Ex-employee   54
  d) Case Study #4, Dirty Revenge   54
- Your Email is a Goldmine to a Skilled Hacker   55
  a) Anatomy of a Hacked Purchase   56

3) **How Hackers Obtain Your Password**   59

If you're not aware how they do it, you can't truly defend against it.

- Watch Someone Type It In   59
- Videotape the Keystrokes   61
- Back Door Access   62
- Within Three Feet of Your Keyboard   64
- Guessing Your Password   65

- Determining Your Password Through Research   **67**
- Use of a Hacking Program with a Hacker's Dictionary   **68**
- Brute Force Hacking Programs   **70**
- Most People Use the Same Password for Everything   **73**
- Simply Open the File and Look   **75**
- Want to Find Out if You've Been Compromised?   **79**
  - a) Who Changed My Password?   **80**
  - b) Footprints in My Email   **81**
  - c) Not from My Computer   **82**

4) How to Create a Hacker-proof Password   **83**

After reading the previous chapters, this will be the jackpot takeaway. Create a password that can't be guessed, can't be calculated, can be unique for every system, and, yes, can even be safely written down!

- Characteristics of a Hacker-proof Password   **85**
- Build a Master Phrase   **87**
- Convert Your Master Phrase into a Master Key   **89**
- Convert Your Master Key into a Variable   **91**
- Create a Pseudo Password Using the Variable   **93**
- Mix and Match for Even Better Security   **97**

5) Identity Theft   **99**

You've heard the warnings and you probably know someone who lost a lot of time and money thanks to some loser stealing their identity. Learn to protect yourself.

- Secure Your Social   **101**
  - a) SSN is the Bullseye   **101**
  - b) Tax Returns   **102**
  - c) Working on Your Behalf   **102**
  - d) SSN Reboot   **103**
- Stealing Your Benefits   **105**
  - a) Borrowing Your Healthcare Benefits   **105**
  - b) Vehicle Insurance Benefits   **105**

c)   Life Insurance Benefits   **106**

d)   Retirement Benefits   **106**

e)   Unemployment Benefits   **106**

- Loaning the Coat Off Your Back   **107**
- Don't be the Low Hanging Fruit   **109**
  a)   Secure that Paper!   **109**
  b)   Protect Your Mail!   **111**
  c)   Check Your Checks   **111**
  d)   Question Authority   **112**
  e)   Get Off the Lists   **114**
  f)   Monitor Your Credit Report   **114**
  g)   Statements that Make a Statement   **116**

6) Other Security Techniques   **119**

This summarizes several additional security techniques.

- Hardware and Software Deterrents   **119**
  a)   Firewall   **119**
  b)   Keep Operating System and Software Updated   **121**
  c)   Back Up Only What You Want to Keep   **122**
  d)   Wipe Before Flushing   **122**
  e)   Default Login   **123**
  f)   Secure Connections   **125**
  g)   Limit File Uploads   **125**
  h)   Remove Form Autofill   **125**
  i)   Security Question Creativity   **126**
  j)   Don't Forget Your Dumb Smartphones   **126**
- PINs   **127**
  a)   Easily Hacked   **127**
  b)   Nifty PIN Idea   **128**
- Transposed Digits   **129**
  a)   Swap Digits   **129**
  b)   Credit Card Considerations   **129**
- How to Report Possible Cyber Crimes and Stolen Identity **133**
  a)   Tax Issues Due to Stolen Identity   **133**

   www.LockingTheCookieJar.com

b)   Report Identity Theft   **133**

c)   Report Cybercrime at the Internet Crime Complaint Center   **133**

Locking the Cookie Jar

How to Protect Against Embezzlement, Identity Theft, and Hackers

This book will teach you how to defend your business and personal life from theft. Not only physical theft, but from electronic and identity theft.

This book starts with a detailed overview of a wide variety of embezzlement schemes. Some smaller businesses will never need to worry about some of these schemes, but at least reviewing the set as a whole can be helpful as you formulate defenses against the more common techniques.

One of the most valuable and unique aspects lies in the sections regarding passwords. Passwords are the primary line of defense for most of your private digital life and the digital assets of your business. You will first learn what hackers value and how they obtain your password, since knowing is the key to defending yourself. Then you will discover a very unique and cool technique to create passwords that meet all of these criteria:

1. Impossible to guess
2. Complex enough to be almost mathematically impossible for hacking programs to decrypt
3. Easy to remember
4. Unique for every single online account
5. And yes, they can even be safely written down!

Who should read this book?

- **Business owners**. Whether you are a sole-proprietor or the CEO of a Fortune 500 company, the information in this book will help you be vigilant when it comes to protecting your business assets and ensuring your IT department is making the right calls. The security of your business is only as strong as the weakest employee link.

Whether that's a rogue employee or one with an easy-to-hack password, the tools in this book can stop a disaster.

- **Anyone with an online account**. If you're like most people, you probably have a dozen or more online accounts (social media, bank, work, email, retailers). If you know how your account can be compromised, you can save yourself a huge headache. And, by learning how a hacker can eventually get your bank accounts and retail logins, you can stop theft.

- **Supervisors**. Your team and company can be hacked because one of your team members has a weak password or habit. Learn how to educate them.

- **Parents and family leaders**. Your family computers, bank accounts, credit ratings, and more can be seriously damaged because a spouse, child, or parent has naïve security. Learn how to protect and educate them. Identity theft is serious and it happens to thousands of people every day who thought it would never happen to them.

Chapter 1
Embezzlement Schemes

"Honesty and integrity are absolutely essential for success in life - all areas of life. The really good news is that anyone can develop both honesty and integrity." – Zig Ziglar[1]

NOTE: If you do not own or manage a business, skip this Chapter!

Do you trust everyone you work with? So did the victims who later read the headlines:

- *"Former Bookkeeper Pleads Guilty of Embezzling More than $40,000 from a New Windsor Business"*
- *"Church Treasurer and Sunday School Teacher Pleads Guilty to Embezzling $80,000 from Baptist Church"*
- *"Former CEO of Kansas Company Pleads Guilty to Stealing $338,221 Over Nine Years"*

The FBI Financial Crimes Report to the Public estimates that financial crimes account for approximately 30%-50% of all business failures.[2]

In the sections that follow, numerous embezzlement schemes are explained. It is critical that you understand that these are not rare occurrences and it would be foolish to assume that your staff won't think of them. These naïve assumptions have been disproved time and time again. Don't be a statistic of failure by blindly trusting your team, and don't tempt them to become a criminal by making embezzlement such an easy thing to do. Build in checks and balances to secure your company and protect the jobs or careers of employees who depend on you.

After each explanation of a type of embezzlement scheme, there is a list of techniques to help combat the types of schemes.

Cash Embezzlement Schemes

Cash embezzlement is one of the most common forms of theft for companies that deal with hard cash (e.g., retail stores, restaurants, food trucks, street vendors). Once money is pocketed, it is difficult to prove the theft unless it was witnessed or you have strict policies that provide enough evidence to convict an employee, even if the theft was not directly witnessed.

Most Common Forms of Cash Embezzlement

- Pocketing cash payments instead of recording them in cash registers or containers. Often the funds will be placed in the container initially, but removed at a convenient time later.
- Stealing cash from unsecured "petty cash" container.
- Overcharging cash-paying customers by a certain dollar amount and later retrieving and pocketing the extra amount.
- Short-changing customers by not giving them back all of the extra cash (change) that is due to them, and later pocketing the extra.
- Stealing cash from personal items left unprotected (purses, backpacks, etc.).
- Stealing cash from another employee's cash drawer.
- Refunding virtual items to virtual customers and pocketing the cash.
- Refunding stolen items for cash. Sometimes this involves an accomplice who might pick an item off your shelf and get a refund for it as if it was paid.
- Funding company gift cards, then using them to buy merchandise as a virtual customer.

Best Techniques to Help Protect Against Cash Embezzlement

- Carefully analyze all steps, evaluate weaknesses, and then develop and enforce written policies and specific procedures governing cash handling, recording, and security.
- Install video cameras from multiple angles. It is important to regularly check video footage and to confront employees that are

suspicious, especially when drawer totals, customer complaints, or other evidence supports a potential impropriety. If you never check footage and it becomes obvious to the staff that you never seem to notice anything on video (even strange customers, spills, etc.), they will ignore it too.

- Require strict dual control over cash drawers, keys, and access.
- Secure all containers used to store or transfer cash. Make sure you can control who has access and when they have access. Bolted-down safes with secure, front deposit mechanisms are excellent tools. Do not give out the combination to anyone who doesn't need to know and change the combination regularly.
- Require that all cash refunds be approved by a supervisor and that refunds over a certain amount be paid via a company check.
- Ensure there is a process to verify gift card loads with payment into the POS to cover that amount.
- Do not allow potential nepotism (i.e., favoritism or partnership by someone in power over a relative or good friend) to exist in a supervisor-subordinate role when it comes to financial duties, as this can lead to a partnership in working around cash management procedures.
- Perform frequent, unannounced drawer counts or cash counts, especially whenever you suspect something or someone. This can catch employees who didn't record a payment, overcharged, or short-changed customers, and haven't removed the extra cash from the drawer yet.

TIPS

One way to test the honesty of cash handlers is to insert or remove cash in their system and see if the overage or underage gets reported accurately. The most important thing about testing this process is to reward the employee if they record it correctly and to have a *very firm* discussion, or decision, if they cover it up. Employees will be a lot more honest about reporting discrepancies, and less likely to pocket the extra or cover the shortage, when they know you might occasionally test them.

- Post a sign with a direct phone number to management telling customers to call if they are not offered a receipt for their payment. Require employees to print the receipt before asking if the customer would like a copy. This avoids having an employee ask before ringing them up, in case they wanted to target those who don't want a copy. A thief can't provide a receipt if they haven't registered the sale in the system.
- Rotate tasks at unpredictable intervals. If employees have begun steps to embezzle but haven't finished the process yet, a sudden change in duties might expose the deed.

AUTHOR SIDEBAR

Our restaurant required a trusted employee to perform a scripted End of Day procedure where, under the coverage of two video cameras, they would count the cash, tips, and credit card receipts. They recorded everything on a pre-printed envelope form we designed. They compared totals to what the POS system reports, recorded differences, sealed receipts and cash in the envelope, signed their name, and then placed it in a secured location. Then one of our managers opened and verified that the contents of the envelope matched a report from the POS. Next, the manager recorded it in a special spreadsheet and prepared a bank deposit with a record of bill totals. Then I verified totals against a separate spreadsheet that I personally populated with cash totals from the envelopes. After bank deposits were made, the bookkeeper would verify that correct totals appeared in the bank account transactions. This allowed inconsistencies to be caught at multiple levels.

Negotiable Document Embezzlement Schemes

A *negotiable document* is a fancy term for something that guarantees payment of a specific amount of money at a set time, usually upon demand. This would apply to documents such as checks, money orders, traveler's checks, credit and debit memos, banknotes, promissory notes, and bills of exchange. To make this simple, let's focus on checks. For most businesses, checks are probably the only thing you have to worry about in this category, but the techniques for securing these other items are similar.

Most Common Forms of Negotiable Document Embezzlement
- Misusing company checks, payroll checks, money orders, and traveler's checks.
- Forgeries or modifications of these types of documents.
- Unauthorized use of credit and debit memos to manipulate accounts.
- Refund authorizations. Some companies require that in order for a customer or employee to get a refund, a refund authorization form must be filled out and sent to the accounting department to provide the refund.

Best Techniques to Help Protect Against Negotiable Document Embezzlement
- Analyze and record the complete process from ordering, receiving, storing, inventory, accessing, recording, and distributing these types of documents. Develop written policies and procedures that deal with each of these steps and require dual control. Ensure that nothing can fall through the cracks, or get pushed through the cracks. For example, you might require that all business checks be ordered through a single person, with a supervisor approval and review, and that a completely different person or department receives them.
- Use security checks with technology that makes it extremely difficult to modify or manipulate. Many careless business owners with weak

reconciliation procedures have fallen prey to manipulated checks and other negotiable documents.

- Rotate tasks at unpredictable intervals. Often designating a new person take over a high-risk task can expose the previous person's devious process.
- Conduct frequent, unannounced audits at unpredictable intervals. Again, this can catch problems before they can get covered up.
- When handling vacations for personnel with high-risk responsibilities, require that they take at least a full week off every year, and do not let them come back during that time. Again, this can expose faulty procedures while they are away and unable to intercept or cover issues.
- Perform occasional tests that insert falsified documents into the system and see if they are caught by your procedures. Reward the catches and fix the loopholes.

Account Credit Embezzlement Schemes

This technique involves the use of specific accounts that are externally accessible by an employee or accomplice, to receive or produce payments or funding. In some of these cases, a fictitious external person or company is setup to receive the money, and this is a lot harder to figure out. However, many of these schemes are not as elaborate and well thought out, and the recipient is simply your employee, their relative, or their side business.

Most Common Forms of Credit Embezzlement
- Creating ghost employee payroll accounts. This is easier to pull off in a company with many employees, but it has occurred in smaller companies. The manipulator activates and deactivates the ghost employee, or a previously-discharged employee. They'll then modify the direct deposit information and employee name at payroll time, and restore it after payroll time.
- Using ghost vendor or client accounts to receive payments based on falsified invoices.
- Sometimes the manipulator has admin access into the accounts payable system and can hide a payment to themselves, or an accomplice, by merely changing the payment transaction after the fact so it shows payment to a different account.
- Transferring funds from inactive or dormant accounts since the owners of the accounts are less likely to notice. Similarly, accessing accounts of the elderly or foreign customers might also go unnoticed.
- Setting up loans and lines of credit for fictitious borrowers.
- Swapping a customer's credit card with a fake or invalid card of the same brand in hopes they don't notice that the numbers and name on the card are different. This allows the employee to go on a shopping spree with the customer's card until the customer figures out their card is still out there and shuts it down.

- Secretly swiping a customer's credit card in a small electronic device that records the magnetic information. This can then be used later to make a duplicate card.
- Writing down a customer's credit card number, expiration date, and security code. This information can then be used to purchase products online or over the phone.
- Using company credit cards, hotel accounts, travel discounts, and company cars for personal use.
- Using company telephones, printers, copy machines, and manufacturing equipment for personal use.
- Lapping scheme. If customer payments are often the same amount as other customers, a wayward employee can be tempted to lap payments to hide embezzlement. When a customer makes a payment, the employee deposits the amount into their own account. Then when another customer makes a payment, the employee uses that payment to pay the first customer's account. Until this cycle is resolved, the employee can't take a leave of absence because they can't afford to have another employee discover their problem. This cycle continues until a situation occurs where either a mistake is made or the employee can allow a problematic customer to get blamed for not paying an old bill.

Best Techniques to Help Protect Against Credit Embezzlement
- Analyze and record the complete process related to credit documents. Develop written policies and procedures that deal with each of these steps and require dual control. Ensure that nothing can fall through the cracks, or get pushed through the cracks. For example, you might require that all new accounts get reviewed and approved by a supervisor before they can be activated.
- Rotate staff, without warning, among the various tasks related to these items.
- Ensure that different people place orders, receive invoices, and make payments on those invoices. This helps avoid letting a thief control the process and cover their tracks without an accomplice.

- Ensure that no one can change payment records after the fact. Or, if you must have this ability, make sure an alert notification gets generated to a higher-level executive and make sure that a read-only transaction log is generated for any such changes.
- Set up a software alert system that notifies managers whenever an inactive account gets accessed.
- Require that a supervisor digitally sign off on account adjustments.
- For customer credit cards, set up a system so the employee never touches the card but instead allows the customer to swipe it themselves. Otherwise ensure there is video coverage at all places that an employee would carry a customer's credit card.
- If a customer reports that they were given back the wrong card, perform a thorough investigation of the situation. Of course, it is possible that a mistake was made but if the errantly-returned card doesn't show up on your history of swiped cards and you can't find a customer name that matches the bad card's name, the hair on the back of your neck should start to stand.
- Do not give out company credit cards unwisely. If you do, ensure the accounts are carefully monitored by supervisors. Also make sure there are strict policies about immediately disabling accounts and collecting cards, keys, and equipment from employees who are suspended or terminated. Many companies require that employees use their own cards and submit expense reports with receipts. This avoids the risk of stolen or misused company cards.
- When hotels and other travel-related companies have corporate accounts, it is essential that travel arrangements only be made through a controlled resource and that careful audits of these accounts are performed.
- Buy copy machines that can create accounts and individual passwords for each employee in order to monitor what they copy.
- Don't forget to monitor the managers too. Some embezzlement schemes are enabled because a manager doesn't need a signoff from someone else in order to make adjustments.
- Perform account audits.

Physical Item Embezzlement Schemes

The most common form of embezzlement pertains to the theft of products or funds based on those products. Not only stealing directly from inventory, but also stealing products arriving through a receiving system or going out through the delivery system.

Most Common Forms of Item Embezzlement
- Property hidden in the garbage, taken out to the exterior garbage container, and then later retrieved from the garbage.
- Removal of raw materials or scrap materials. Even something as small a removing scrap wiring or bad circuit boards can add up in potential losses because there is value in recycling the precious metals in the circuit boards or the copper in the wire.
- Removing money or items involved in a layaway program.
- Shipping products to an employee's home or to the location of an accomplice.
- Removing received products and not recording that they were received.
- Using an employee discount to benefit friends.
- Theft of equipment, supplies, or services. Everything from stealing the physical equipment and supplies to using the equipment, supplies, or services for non-work projects.
- Items held in trust.
- Physical stocks, bonds, and negotiable items.

Best Techniques to Help Protect Against Item Embezzlement
- Analyze and record the complete processes related to physical items. Develop written policies and procedures that deal with receiving products, shipping products, and storing items. Attempt to build in and require dual control for each step. Ensure that nothing can fall through the cracks, or get pushed through the cracks. For example, you might require that all external garbage areas are secured by a

key and video surveillance to discourage employees from attempting to steal items through the garbage process.

- Perform frequent inventory counts to ensure that all items are accounted for. If items are missing, they were likely stolen by a customer or employee sometime between this inventory time or the last time you did an inventory. Oh, by the way, don't have the same employees who had the easiest opportunity to steal be the ones doing the inventory! This would allow them to give a false inventory count to cover their tracks.

- Install video surveillance systems in all areas that might be subject to physical embezzlement.

- For shipping products out, some companies have one employee pack the box, another prepare the shipping label, and another verify the label on the box is accurate right before it gets put on the truck. This reduces the chance of someone adding extra items to the box or preparing an alternate shipping label.

- Secure the storage areas where physical items are kept and, depending on the situation, require multiple keys or access codes in order to access those areas.

- Require that items being purchased by an employee are opened by the cashier and inspected before they are bagged and taken. This will lessen the chance that the employee was able to place other items inside the package before purchasing.

- Rotate shipping and receiving tasks among personnel at random intervals.

www.LockingTheCookieJar.com

Computer-based Embezzlement Schemes

The most common embezzlement schemes involving computer software require a little bit of technical know-how, but they can be effective and sometimes difficult to discover. These crimes are usually committed by data processing staff, software developers, or unauthorized access to computer system by either internal or external methods. The ultimate goal in these schemes is to steal identity, accounts and passwords, funds, property, products, or to cause problems with the computer system. The person trying to cause problems is often a disgruntled employee or ex-employee, or a hacker getting kicks out of wreaking havoc.

Most Common Forms of Computer-based Embezzlement
- Skimming funds out of customer accounts into another account. Often this involves dormant accounts, or modifying certain types of transactions as they are applied. Even something as small as a five-cent skim doesn't sound like much, but imagine if that amount was skimmed once a month for a million accounts!
- Stealing account information for the purposes of identity theft.
- Removing security barriers or building workarounds in the system.
- *Trojan horse* programmatic code that hides dormant inside software until a certain condition occurs (e.g., on a specific date and time, a particular type of transaction is recognized, and a hidden signal is sent to it). Often the Trojan horse hides behind security and when it strikes, it can make the computer perform all kinds of functions including transferring funds or data, creating logins, covering its own tracks, deleting data, shutting down or crashing the system, etc.
- Abusing the high-level security access that many programmers possess to access data programmatically. This can be by the programmer himself or through his account and password that was shared or hacked.
- Using computer systems, databases, and connections for personal use. For example, a sheriff's office employee might use the license

plate to find the address of an idiot who cut them off on the roadway, or a healthcare worker might try to look up the confidential health records of a celebrity or neighbor.

- A growing form of external computer-based embezzlement is *ransomware*. Ransomware is malicious software that blocks access to a computer system, data, or features until a ransom is paid to unblock it. Sometimes it includes a threat to publish the data or delete the data. Some ransomware can be removed but some uses a technique called cryptoviral extortion which encrypts the victim's files until an untraceable digital currency (e.g., Bitcoin) is paid as ransom. Ransomware often starts as a Trojan horse but the "WannaCry worm" is a high-profile virus that traveled between computers without user interaction.

Best Techniques to Help Protect Against Computer-based Embezzlement

- Analyze and record the complete processes related to your computer systems. Make sure you can record and control access to sensitive databases, administer terminals, source code for custom software, and security rights, including how they are setup, modified, and terminated. Develop written policies and procedures that deal with key security aspects of your computer systems and login access. Attempt to build in and require dual control for risky steps and access. Ensure that nothing can fall through the cracks, or get pushed through the cracks.
- Password security is critical! You must educate staff about using secure account names and passwords and require that complex passwords be used and changed often. Assigning accounts and adding a third level of security access, such as a key fob or a digital timer that changes access codes by the minute, can significantly boost security. Require that all staff, even interns, have login accounts to the system so no one can use the computers unless they can login to the computers. Also require that all users are carefully assigned appropriate levels of access clearance pertaining to their job responsibilities.

- Perform regular full backups of data and incremental backups of data in between. Develop a backup storage system offsite in the event of a virus, data corruption, data deletion, or even a building disaster such as a fire, flood, or a local drunk driving his truck into the side of your building. Don't laugh, these have all happened before, and many of these businesses didn't recover from the data loss. Many companies actually create detailed disaster-recovery plans with the ability to move their data center to another location should something devastating happen. It's so much easier to plan these details before disaster happens. By the way, don't store the only copy of these plans inside your data center!
- Require key swipe access to any areas that are sensitive. This includes your Information Technology Department, the room(s) housing main computers, an air conditioning system that cools the data center, onsite and offsite data storage, and any other areas that might be sensitive to the operation of your data center (e.g., main electrical room).
- Routinely monitor and audit all employee access levels. Many times, employees change roles within the company and access levels are not changed accordingly.
- If your company develops custom or commercial software, you should set up a source code library for the source code. Enforce strict procedures regarding the checking out of source code for modification, careful review of the source code, and testing of modifications in a separate, secure *sandbox*, by a different programmer before allowing into a live environment.
- Make sure your system securely stores activity logs and frequently audit those logs, looking for inconsistencies and odd behavior such as attempts to access secure data, repeated attempts at logging in, and access to systems that the employee should not be accessing.
- Educate your staff to avoid clicking on attachments in unknown or unexpected emails or visiting websites that are not mainstream. The power of "the click" can significantly damage your company if the

click activates malware. An unwise or fooled employee can be the weak link to making your whole computer system vulnerable.

Summary of Effective Deterrents to Embezzlement

"With over 20 years of experience in Loss Prevention, I believe that the risk of internal theft is highest when employees perceive a lack of awareness with management. The prevention of internal theft can be directly linked to regular audits, surprise audits, and the sharing of details around the audit results. Opportunity + Desire = Theft. If you take the opportunity away, and employees understand the consequences associated with dishonest acts, the risk of internal theft is minimized." – Christie Harrison, Loss Prevention Professional and Certified Forensic Interviewer (C.F.I.)

It can be difficult to stop extremely determined and motivated embezzlers. However, here are some general techniques that employers can implement to make it less attractive and higher risk for an employee tempted to be naughty. Some of these items are mentioned above but they are repeated here because they are generally very helpful to dissuade many forms of embezzlement.

- The number one deterrent is the careful analysis of all steps of a process, and then developing policies and procedures to fix weak areas in order to help protect your company. This concept is listed in the first bullet point of each set of deterrent techniques listed above. These policies and procedures need to be a series of checks and balances in your procedures so that, as much as possible, no single employee has the ability to steal without recruiting the help of an accomplice. But having a policy and procedure book gathering dust on a shelf isn't enough. You must thoroughly train your staff, enforce the procedures, and have serious consequences when procedures are sidestepped.

- Add recorded video coverage to exterior building doors and all sensitive areas such as cash registers, inventory storage, data centers, exterior garbage bins, and restrooms (just checking to see if you were paying attention). There are many affordable video systems available and some of the newer consumer features blow away many of the expensive systems of only a decade ago. Make sure video cameras record into a *secured* storage location (so thieves can't remove or destroy the evidence), with battery backup (so thieves can't cut power to turn off the recording). Implement a system that stores recorded videos for as long as reasonable in the event you need to go back in time to collect more evidence or find a pattern of theft. Most importantly, spend time to check your footage! You can't catch crime if you don't see it happening. Anytime you suspect something, pull up that video, put it on fast forward, and look for what you suspect.

AUTHOR SIDEBAR

At our restaurant, I was able to pull up footage from video cameras to provide proof to the local police department when our tip jar was stolen. We caught two thieves (different incidents) stealing this puppy right in front of our staff.

I've also used it to justify letting an employee "have the opportunity to work elsewhere" because their "work habits" were repeatedly caught on video. It's pretty solid evidence that makes firing decisions a lot easier when the proof is irrefutable. You'd think that the deterrent of just knowing that the cameras are present should be enough; but when it isn't for a particular employee, it might be time for that gene pool to move to another pond.

- Depending on your business, perform background checks on employees and require that they get fingerprinted. This can alert you to past convictions of theft, violence, sexual predator crimes, and other characteristics that you might want to consider before inviting them to be on your team and access vital areas of your business.

WARNING ⚠

Lie detectors, also known as polygraph tests, or "psychological stress evaluator tests," used to be fairly common tools for employers to evaluate employees before hiring. Some employers, however, fell into the tempting trap of asking about extremely private matters while the poor applicant was strapped in and had to make the very stressful decision to either answer or walk away from the job. This abuse spurred the federal Employee Polygraph Protection Act that was passed in 1988. This act essentially outlawed polygraph tests for most businesses. However, the act does not apply to employees of federal, state, or local government. It also does not apply to certain jobs related to national defense, employees in security, the handling of controlled drugs, or to suspects of an employee-related crime. Even in the case of these exceptions, there are strict rules governing how the test is performed. These regulations vary slightly by state.

- Businesses can also require drug testing on employees as long as they are consistent. While this lifestyle can exist outside of work, it often affects employees at work when they are under the influence of drugs while operating equipment, driving company vehicles, etc. In regards to embezzlement, employers must understand that a drug lifestyle can sometimes be accompanied by the need to obtain extra cash to fund their habit, especially when it becomes an addiction.

- Unannounced audits, spot checks, and role switching can catch someone before they have time to cover up their tracks. At the very least, it will keep employees on their toes and lessen the temptation because of the increased risk of getting caught.

- Depending on how you structure your organization, it might be wise to disallow nepotism. Do not hire relatives or best friends of employees, and do not allow employees to have a supervisory chain over a relative or best friend. This not only invites favoritism (or extra harsh treatment, depending on the situation outside the office), but it sets up a situation that allows for much easier partnerships in crime. Of course, if you are a small family business, this type of policy will probably not work for you.

- When it comes to bookkeeping security, the owners need to be proactive. Carrying an attitude of slight distrust towards your bookkeeper might feel uncomfortable, but it can save your business if you are diligent about spot checking work. At a very minimum, you or another trusted partner in the business should regularly review the books and question transactions, accounts, or receipts that are not understood or seem strange.

- If you are able to split the duties between different people, it always a good idea to separate the responsibility of recording transactions in the system with the responsibilities of actually making payments, signing checks, making bank deposits, etc. This makes it much more difficult for one person to, for example, write a check to themselves but record that it was paid to a vendor. Also, the person writing checks probably should not be the person reconciling the checking account later. For this reason, many bookkeepers do not have full access to bank accounts, other than being able to view and print bank transactions.

SOURCES

For more information and a list of helpful resources, companies, and products, that can help you better secure your business, scan this barcode or go to:

www.LockingTheCookieJar.com/resources-bk

Chapter 2
Hacking the Hacker's Mind

"A common mistake that people make when trying to design something completely foolproof is to underestimate the ingenuity of complete fools."
– Douglas Adams

Hacker by Definition

The technical definition for *hacker* is, "A person who uses computers to gain unauthorized access to data." Synonyms include cybercriminal, pirate, computer criminal, keylogger, cyberpunk, and hacktivist.

The term "hacker" conjures up thoughts of high-level computer experts that sit at an orchestra of computer monitors surrounding their desks in the basement of a secured building. Outside of Hollywood, there are a relatively few of these highly-skilled experts in the world, and the targets they go after are high-level and will result in lucrative payoffs for someone. Governments, high-level crime rings, military branches, very large companies, and other wealthy entities might employ these folks. The good news is that the chances that you or your company will ever be in their crosshairs is unlikely.

There are two camps of hackers:

1. **White hat hackers.** These folks actually do their trade to catch criminals, right wrongs, monitor enemies, and protect assets. It takes one to know one and the best white hats used to wear a darker shade at one point in the past.

2. **Black hat hackers.** These folks do their trade to steal, terrorize, destroy, and take advantage of others. Many of these folks do it for their own self-fulfillment.

White hat hackers might be considered law enforcement and modern-day Robin Hoods. Black hat hackers are the lowest form of life as far as their victims are concerned. Many of the black hats do it for the fun of the challenge, similar to solving a puzzle. A stereotypical description of a black hat hacker could be, an unethical computer programmer who still lives with his mother and sits around in his boxers eating Cheetos while playing World of Warcraft on one screen and breaking into personal accounts on another screen.

The Majority of Bottom Feeders

Most hackers around the world go after the login of a specific type of software system. The reason they want this access is so they can get easy pay for advertising. Lucky for the victim, this type of hacker is short-sighted as to the value of what they possess.

For example, the hacker signs up as an affiliate advertiser or is hired by an affiliate advertiser to help them get paid for affiliate marketing. Their goal is to get people to click on a specific link, which will provide the affiliate advertiser with a small payment. The more people that click, the higher the total payment. The hacker knows that the best way to get someone to click on a link is to have their friend suggest it. The hacker goes after their login so he can use it to promote the ads to the victim's friends. For this scenario, the process is usually automated and it starts with a Trojan horse approach to harvest accounts and passwords.

Trojan Horses Start as Innocent Ponies
The Greeks left behind a large, hollow wooden statue of a horse when they pretended to abandon Troy. This weapon allowed the hidden warriors inside to attack Troy when they didn't expect it.

Black hat hackers use a software version of a Trojan horse to infect your computer. You think you're opening a video file or installing a new app but the program is secretly infecting your computer with a program that can do all kinds of damage including destroying data, copying data to the Internet, sending emails to all your friends, and much more.

Phishing for Phools
A fisherman fishes for his prey by dangling a piece of safe-looking food in front of an unsuspecting victim. Phishing is a technique that essentially convinces a victim that he is logging into a safe location, yet is really logging into a fake web page that collects his login information.

Here's a sample phishing technique that most people can identify with: You get an email from "your bank" that says there is a problem that you need to fix with your account (e.g., it's overdrawn, a huge check just cleared, it has been frozen, etc.). The email includes a link for you to jump to the banking system. You click the link and the website that appears looks just like your bank login page, so you login. After logging in, you might receive a message about having the wrong password and then you get redirected to the real login page, where you try it again and get through. Or you might end up just sitting there on the page as it does nothing. Behind the scenes, the fake login screen stored your account name and password in a file. Later, it will be used to login to your bank account.

How can you tell when you are being phooled? The easiest way is to consider their claim. Are you expecting your bank account to be overdrawn? Are you expecting a huge check to clear? Why would there be something wrong with your PayPal account? Does the IRS really communicate via email?

Hovering over the link can be a helpful clue. If you are expecting to be on the Amazon website and it doesn't show amazon.com somewhere in the address, something is wrong and you should not trust it. Likewise, if you don't see chase.com in the address bar of your browser when you're expecting to be on Chase's website, do not trust the source. Beware of similar-looking websites. Seeing www.amazon-com/blah-blah/mudjunk.com should trigger the thought, "It's amazon-com instead of amazon.com! DO NOT trust it!"

AUTHOR SIDEBAR

During my senior year of college as a computer science student, I turned in a senior project related to encryption and password security. While I was proud of the super cool "discretely-random matrix" encryption algorithm I designed, my professor was most interested in the separate 20-page report that I handed in. It was a list of most of the computer accounts and passwords on campus! It was not just student accounts, it was faculty and the system operator too. I highlighted the SysOp's account with a yellow highlighter. The other yellow highlight was my professor's account and password. I wrote in a smiley face next to his.

I told him when I started my project that I was going to figure out how to accomplish this and he chuckled in disbelief. The first page was a signed affidavit stating that I swore I never accessed any account, other than the System Operator's account, which I used to create a few fake, high-level accounts to run my hack.

As soon as I printed the only copy of this report, I immediately deleted the fake accounts and then used the SysOp's account to delete some log file history (to remove evidence in case someone found out, didn't appreciate it, and wanted proof to get me in trouble before graduation).   (continued...)

AUTHOR SIDEBAR

The report was sorted by password, which proved my point that most users selected easy-to-guess passwords. It was shocking how many passwords were duplicated when the users thought they were so creative.

How did I obtain these passwords? First, let's set the scene. This was in the '80s when only a few students had PCs. Most computer-related work was performed on the campus's minicomputer, which was anything but "mini." To access the computer, you'd log into one of the many green screen terminals around campus.

At the time, I referred to my technique as a Trojan horse technique because the "phishing" term hadn't been coined yet. I got the idea from experiencing a static-sensitive set of terminals located in the carpeted basement of the library. At random times while logged into one of these terminals, moving your feet on the carpet could cause a static shock if the user touched the terminal. This common occurrence would make the screen flash and would then reset the terminal and the login screen would reappear, thus losing your unsaved work.

(continued...)

---

www.LockingTheCookieJar.com

AUTHOR SIDEBAR

3 of 4

I sat down and wrote a computer program that looked exactly like the login screen of the minicomputer's terminals. After the user would enter their account name and password, the program would randomly do one of two things. It would display an error message saying that the password was incorrect and would then go back to the login screen, or it would flash the screen and return to the login screen.

What the user didn't realize is that when they first sat down, they were seeing the fake login screen of my program. When they'd enter their account and password, my program would save it to a file and then either flash or show a fake "incorrect password" notification, and then terminate. This would then bring up the real login screen.

The user would either think they mistyped their password or that they were a victim of static. Either way, they'd carefully type it in the second time, on the real login screen, and would get access as expected. They had no idea that their account and password were recorded.

(continued...)

AUTHOR SIDEBAR

4 of 4

Because I was a computer science major, I was frequently in these terminal rooms doing my work. Whenever someone got up and left, I'd slide over to the terminal, run my program, and the trap would be set for the next victim.

It took about a week before I snagged the System Operator's password. Once I found that in my database, I got to work. I immediately used his "God account" to create four new accounts. Two were regular student accounts that wouldn't draw any suspicion. I used these accounts to run the program so my real account would no longer be used (couldn't be traced). The two other accounts were high-level operator accounts that allowed me to create users, move files between accounts, and delete some of the log files to cover my tracks.

I had to use the SysOp's account to completely hide my tracks, but I risked him discovering that his account was being used if he tried logging in while I was logged in. Therefore, I only used his account rarely, and only late at night when he wasn't on site.

What Kind of Damage Can a Hacker Impose?

Many people do not realize that hackers can do a lot more than just destroy your computer files. Some are surprised to learn that a skilled hacker can use the information found on your computer to do the following:

- Access and use your credit cards to make purchases
- Harvest your email accounts to discover important info
- Slowly drain your bank accounts or quickly wire transfer funds
- Steal (more like borrow) your identity
- Hijack your social media accounts and wreak havoc on your relationships and reputation
- Access, steal, modify, or destroy the data you can access on your employer's systems
- Destroy your career
- Force you into bankruptcy and serious legal challenges

Below is a series of case studies that show just how serious this situation can be.

Case Study #1, Goodbye Retirement

Throughout his career, Henry worked hard to build up his retirement account. When he was only three years away from retiring comfortably, he received a shocking letter from the company that managed his 401K. It showed that his account dropped from seven digits to four digits! After researching the transactions, he discovered that someone logged into his account and sold off all of his stock and mutual funds and then bought junk stock on margin. The hacker didn't attempt to borrow or withdraw any of the funds. The goal was clearly to destroy Henry's retirement.

Case Study #2, Healthcare Confidentiality... NOT

Veronica worked as a triage nurse at the community hospital where she ignored company policy by using an easy-to-guess password. A young hacker used her account to access the medical records of all patients that came through the emergency room. After the most embarrassing medical situations were posted on the Internet, including the patient names and addresses, a class action lawsuit not only hurt the hospital's reputation, but caused the firing of two of the executive staff and Veronica.

Case Study #3, Disgruntled Ex-employee

Bernie was a disgruntled ex-employee of a popular restaurant. Shortly after he was let go, he discovered that the management didn't remove his login from the company's event reservation system. He was hell-bent on seeking revenge and decided to punish his former employer. With help from a hacker friend, Bernie was able to download about a year's worth of reservation information, which included complete customer credit card numbers, addresses, and emails. Bernie then bought thousands of dollars of items from dozens of different online stores and shipped the products to the restaurant and the homes of the management. He also used the reservation system to email out offensive and insulting messages to these customers. Bernie and his hacker friend were caught and jailed, but the damage was done and the restaurant lost the trust of most of these patrons.

Case Study #4, Dirty Revenge

Richard got revenge on a coworker, Dave, who backstabbed him at work. He figured out Dave's password and accessed his email account where he learned all kinds of information. He started by cancelling all kinds of services to Dave's home. He cancelled Dave's home and car insurance, electricity, phone, trash pickup, and pool service. He then posted social media messages and emailed Dave's entire contact list with a false message that talked about Dave's recent marital problems and his spouse's affair. He told everyone that "he" (Dave) was getting a divorce and that he'd appreciate it if everyone would delete him from their contact lists because he wants to break all ties. Then Richard changed the passwords on all of Dave's social media accounts and then finished his revenge by deleting Dave's email account!

Your Email is a Goldmine to a Skilled Hacker

For a serious hacker, the password to your email account is the initial goal. Many email systems require only two pieces of information to be accessed: the email address and the password. The email address is simple. We know our friend's email addresses since we can't send them anything without it. Email addresses are on business cards, websites, Facebook, and in our electronic address books, our inboxes, and our friends' inboxes. The only other piece of information a hacker needs is your password.

The Holy Grail on a serious hacker's quest is the password of your email. We'll discuss how he obtains that password later. Once a hacker can access your email, your private world is at the mercy of a stranger who doesn't care about you.

By examining your email, a hacker can find out information like:

- Where you live
- Where you work
- Who your friends are
- Where you bank
- Where you like to shop online (Amazon, Wal-Mart, eBay, PayPal, credit cards, etc.)
- Whether or not you tend to open emailed receipts and notifications from online shopping stores
- When you typically use your email

Most of these are obvious but that last one, "when" you use your email, is a powerful piece of knowledge. By examining your Sent folder, the hacker can see the times that you typically reply and send out email. Let's assume that you tend to use your email on weekdays between 7:30 a.m. and 8:00 p.m. This means that the hacker can safely work in your email late at night and possibly on weekends. (Remember the Author's Sidebar above when SysOp's email was accessed late at night so he wouldn't notice?)

With this knowledge, the hacker can use some sneaky techniques to buy products using your existing online account at your favorite online store. Here's how:

Anatomy of a Hacked Purchase

A hacker would first attempt to login to one of your online retail accounts that allows you to save your credit card information. He'd login during a time that you typically don't use your email account. He'd login using your email and hacked password since he knows you probably use the same password for everything.

To safely buy from your account, he'd first change your shipping address to a friend's house or a business in which he controls incoming shipments. Some brave, but dumb, hackers might use their own address but this is highly dangerous.

He would then buy products using your stored credit card. When the receipt arrives in your inbox (order complete), he'd go back into the online store and change back the address. He'd quickly delete the receipt from your inbox, and then delete from your Deleted folder. If your email system allows rules to be created, the hacker can create a rule that monitors for shipping status updates and either deletes them or moves them to a folder that you can clear out late at night.

Another technique is for the hacker to temporarily change the email associated with the retail account to point to a junk one that he controls. Then, after the package arrives, he can change the email back to the owner. This lets him cover his tracks better.

This technique doesn't work for every online retailer and retailers are trying to build in features to make this more difficult. However, variations of this technique will often work on online systems as long as the hacker controls your email account.

If a really sharp hacker has gained access to your purchasing ability, he will sometimes try to slowly milk you over time instead of butcher you all at once. He knows that if he gets crazy with big purchases, you're going to notice that your Visa bill suddenly changed from $2,000 per month to $5,000 per month. You'll probably also notice if there are dozens of extra charges on your billing statement as opposed to your typical number of charges.

Another technique is to find a charge towards the end of your previous billing cycle and attempt to buy something for about the same price at the beginning of the current cycle. Using this technique, they hope that in the event you do notice the purchase a month from now, you might ignore it by thinking it was the purchase they made in the billing period before that.

Therefore, if they see that you tend to ignore receipt emails and if they can tell whether or not you have autopay setup for your credit card statement, they might attempt to bleed you slowly over time in hopes that you're lazy and don't bother to check the details of your credit card statement on a regular basis.

When you don't notice a few extra purchases, you're a perfect victim. Imagine the buying power that a hacker can have if they find a dozen lazy sugar daddies from which to steal.

Chapter 3
How Hackers Obtain Your Password

There are many ways to figure out someone's password. Some are so simple that they are almost laughable. Yet with each scenario listed below, incredible damage has occurred to individuals, small businesses, large corporations, and governments.

Watch Someone Type It In

Watching someone type in their password is incredibly easy to do. Many corporate executives have fallen victim to this easy technique, sometimes with the bad guy standing right next to them in their office. You'd think that people would protect their password to every extent possible but far too many people just assume that no one would actually watch them type it in.

Several students in a high school classroom decided that they wanted access to their teacher's grade book system. They knew that the teacher's daily classroom habit of walking into class and immediately signing into his desktop computer was the key. Because the teacher typed quickly, it was difficult to figure out all of the letters at once, but by listening, they knew it was nine key presses before he pressed the Enter key. It took them several days to figure it out but they worked as a team by taking turns standing at his desk when he walked in and logged in. They got the first two letters on the first attempt: "li" followed by a key on the left side of the keyboard. On the second day, a different student stood nearby and listened for the third keystroke while watching the left side of the keyboard and saw that it appeared to be an "f." At lunch they talked about those first three letters, "lif," and theorized that the next letter would be an "e" to spell "life." Sure enough, when tomorrow came, the student watched the "e" key and saw it get pressed on the 4th keystroke, followed by and "s" and possibly a "y" or a "u." At the next class, the spy clearly saw that the last three letters were "cks" and that evening, they hacked into the grading system with the password of "lifesucks." Life did suck for both the teacher and the students once the situation was discovered.

Some password heists are a little sneakier and less obvious. For example, a high-powered telescope has been used to observe the login process of top executives. Executives who sit at their desks with their backs to the window can be victimized by a thief setup in a neighboring building. The telescope is used to watch the keyboard much the same way the students observed their teacher above. Binoculars, zoom camera lenses, and even a child's pirate telescope have been used to heist passwords and read confidential emails over the shoulder of executives who think the beautiful skyline behind them is a safe haven.

Passwords are not the only target. PINs, lock combinations, key pad entry codes, and more can be targeted with direct observation. Be careful when typing, turning, and pushing numbers. Always assume someone is watching.

Videotape the Keystrokes

Capitalizing on the watch techniques above, the ultimate observation tool is video. Smartphones, small computers, digital cameras, security systems, and other devices can often carry very powerful video capabilities.

For many years, video has been used to record countless manually-entered codes. That teen behind you at the grocery store who is looks like he's texting on his cellphone might be secretly taping your credit card number and expiration date as you hold the card in your hand, in hopes that you'll also show the back of the card to the video camera, exposing the security code too.

The HD video surveillance system in your office quadrant might provide your login information to a security technician. This recording can be used later to access the system "as you." It is critical that anyone wanting to secure passwords, PINs, and combinations, take on a suspicious defense when cameras are around or might be around. Video and photographs have even been used to get a clear-enough image of a key, that a duplicate key can be created by filing a blank key to match the image. This is serious stuff.

Back Door Access

Programmers who develop access systems often know how to get through the systems. This is very difficult to control since they have access to the source code, algorithms, and procedures developed around the security systems. In order to properly test these systems, they often build back doors and side doors into the code so they can test specific sections of the code.

AUTHOR SIDEBAR

I used to lead a high-tech software development team that developed software that needed to have password encryption technology that would hold up in court in the event a digital signature was challenged.

We created a high-level encryption and decryption program that was essentially un-hackable by all but the highest level of nerds. We secured access to the source code and built in some tricky techniques so that even someone accessing the compiled code would have a difficult time figuring out how it operated and how to use it. However, myself and some of our top programmers knew how the algorithm worked, and we knew how to use the compiled programs so they would function.

My team was highly ethical, but I'm sure some executives would be surprised to learn that most of us could access anything we wanted to access inside the system.

Sometimes the knowledge of a backdoor access can be too much for a programmer to keep secret. Bragging about the knowledge or proving it to someone they want to impress can be very tempting for some developers who lack self-esteem, ethics, or are listening too closely to The Dark Side.

Many systems have built-in default passwords. These exist for initial startup and configuration processes. Although the instructions clearly say to delete the account or change the password after a regular login account has been created, many times this step is forgotten or ignored. Thousands of incidents of theft have occurred because people didn't follow instructions and change the default password to something different. Novell networking systems used to have this problem as well as some high-level accounting systems, routers, and mainframe computers.

There was a case involving some hackers who drove their car down the street slowly with their laptop turned on and looked at the routers in the neighborhood. When they'd find one from a certain manufacturer, they'd try logging in with the default password. In many cases, they'd get onto the network and access shared drives and devices because the owners didn't change the default password to something unique. This same technique has allowed hackers to easily login at large corporate headquarters, because no one thought to remove the default account. In some cases, they created a separate account for themselves so that once the default one was deleted, they could still access the system as desired.

Decision makers who are concerned about backdoor access to their internal systems need to ask questions to determine how the backdoor access works and how it can be closed. If the lingo is over their head, they should find a qualified techie to help interview the development manager and possibly check some source code to understand the security risks. Be aware that you do not want to create a new security risk by "opening the kimono" to a consultant, so work with your development manager to ensure the information shared won't allow a rogue consultant to access your system later.

Within Three Feet of Your Keyboard

Most adults write their passwords on a piece of paper. Over half of all adults "hide" this valuable piece of paper within three feet of their keyboard, both at home and at their office. The hilarious thing is that most of these hiding places are directly underneath your keyboard! Golly, and you thought no one knew?

The most lucrative thing that a "smart" thief (yeah, it's an oxymoron) could steal from your home or your office is not your jewelry or electronic equipment. If they could merely take a photo of your password list so you didn't even realize it was taken, they might be able to steal far more than the worth of your assets in your home or office.

Just imagine what could eventually be stolen from you if you didn't know your passwords were taken!

Guessing Your Password

The sad reality is that most people use easy-to-guess passwords. Chances are, you do too. The funny thing is that most people who use these passwords secretly feel that they are original thinkers and that no one could ever guess the password.

According to the New York Post, the twenty-five most stolen passwords include:[3]

1. 123456
2. password
3. 12345678
4. Qwerty (the top row of left keys on your keyboard)
5. 12345
6. 123456789
7. football
8. 1234
9. 1234567
10. baseball
11. welcome
12. 1234567890
13. abc123
14. 111111
15. 1qaz2wsx
16. dragon
17. master
18. monkey
19. letmein
20. login
21. princess
22. qwertyuiop (the top row of keys on your keyboard)
23. solo
24. passw0rd

25. starwars

If you are like most people, you will recognize a few of these passwords as something you currently use or have used in the past...right? If these don't look familiar to you, then bravo! You are above average in the security arena.

Most hackers want low-hanging fruit. Unless they are focused on you specifically, they will try several of these passwords and if they can't break through with one, they will often give up and move along to someone else's account.

Determining Your Password Through Research

When a hacker targets a specific victim, they can often find success by doing a little background research on the victim. Motivated hackers will take the time to research their victim. This research can significantly increase the chances of figuring out their password.

Here is a partial list of background information that some people use to create their "foolproof" password:

- First, middle, last, and maiden names of family members
- Pet names, boyfriend/girlfriend names
- Past and current street addresses, phone numbers, license plates
- Birthdates, anniversaries, graduations
- Favorite sports teams, athletes
- Birth cities, states, childhood towns, schools
- Bands, musicians, movies, books, employers, etc.
- Local Terms: local sports teams, stars, cities, landmarks

The key for a hacker is to study the victim carefully through social media, Google, phone calls, direct contact, and other avenues in this realm.

Use of a Hacking Program with a Hacker's Dictionary

Technical hackers who are determined will often use a hacking program. Obviously these programs are not for sale on Amazon but they can be written by skilled programmers.

This program essentially gets set up to access a targeted database. Sometimes the program controls just the login screen and sometimes it directly controls the database behind the login screen. It can repeatedly attempt to access an account, or a list of accounts, using a list of passwords.

The essential ingredient to success is finding a login system that won't lock up after a certain number of incorrect password attempts. Remember that the vast majority of people use the same password for multiple accounts, so why would a hacker attempt to target your bank login when they only get three tries before being locked out and notifying the victim that a hack attempt was made? Instead, the hacker would rather go after the same password from your low-security gaming account.

This list of passwords to be used against the account can be taken directly out of a hacker's dictionary or they can be programmatically generated.

A good hacker's dictionary can be a powerful tool. There are about 30,000 words in the English dictionary. A high-speed connection and fast login script can run through a whole dictionary in just a few minutes. Top-notch hackers often develop their own custom dictionary. A good "hacking dictionary" contains all English words spelled forwards and backwards, with 123, 12345, 321, 54321, 1, 2, 3, and other digits added to the words. It contains popular passwords, phrases, dates, and words from foreign dictionaries. They sort the database by most popular use down to least popular use. If the hacker is targeting a specific victim, they will create an additional addendum containing person-specific words, phrases, and dates through techniques described earlier.

The hacking program merely tries the first word listed in the dictionary. If it fails, it tries the second word, then the third, and so forth until it either gains access to the account or it runs out of words. The vast majority of passwords can be discovered this way.

Brute Force Hacking Programs

If the hacker's dictionary fails, the hacker may resort to the brute force method of programmatically-generated passwords. Given an infinite amount of time and computing power, ANY password could be discovered using this technique. Governments use this technique. In simple terms, it basically tries every possible combination of characters until it discovers the password.

The hacker starts by creating a character list containing all characters that could be used in a password. A basic character list would include all the characters you find on your keyboard. In 99.9% of all cases, this is enough to calculate the password as described below. For trickier passwords or international victims, the hacker can expand the character list to include hundreds or thousands of the many special characters you don't normally see on the keyboard such as "£," "Ӿ," and "⊣." But again, it is extremely rare that a targeted victim would actually use characters not found on the keyboard.

To describe this in as simple an example as possible, let's pretend that the entire alphabet consists of only the letters "abc" instead of the several hundreds or thousands of characters it really contains. Let's also pretend that the hacker knows that the password size has to be exactly three characters. Again, this knowledge is just to make this example easier to follow. Let's pretend that the unknown password is "bac" and the hacker is using "abc" character list to find it.

The brute force hacking program uses the character list (abc) and starts by trying "aaa" then "aab" then "aac" then "aba" and the rest looks like this: abb, abc, aca, acb, acc, baa, bab, and when it tries "bac" it discovers the match!

Of course, this requires a system that does not have a lockout feature if the correct password is not provided in a certain number of tries.

It is important to understand that working through every possible combination of characters in a large character list can be extremely time intensive for a person, but this is what computers excel at. However, even super computers get bogged down when they attempt to perform a brute force hack on a long password.

For example, if the character list only contains numerals (0-9), then a 1-digit password has 10 possible combinations. A 2-digit password has 100 possible combinations (00 through 99). A 3-digit password has 1000 possible combinations (000 through 999). A 5-digit password would have 100,000 combinations, and a 6-digit password would have 1,000,000 combinations. If you jump to a 10-digit password, it results in 10,000,000,000 (ten billion) combinations. At this level, it can take a computer quite a bit of time to calculate every possible combination.

Now let's see what happens if we increase our character list to contain every possible keyboard character, which is 95 characters for most keyboards. If the password is just one character long, then there are obviously 95 possible answers. If the password is two characters long, then there are 9,025 possible combinations. If the password is five characters long, then the possible solutions leaps to 7,737,809,375 different possibilities. Are you sitting down? If the password is increased to 10 characters in length, the brute force method has to try up to 59,873,693,923,837,890,625 possible combinations! Even a room full of super computers would choke on this number of possibilities.

Just for fun, let's increase our character list to contain not only every possible keyboard character, but also the whole ASCII list (all characters that can be made with Alt key sequences, explained in a sidebar). This is a list of 254 possible characters. If the password is five characters long, there are 1,057,227,821,024 different possibilities. However, if the user created a password with 10 characters in it, the brute force program would have to try up to a whopping 1,117,730,665,547,154,976,408,576 different combinations of characters in order to figure out the password!

What's the takeaway? The longer you make your password and the more exotic types of characters you use in the password, the less likely you'll be to have to publicly apologize for "sharing" obscene videos on Facebook.

SOURCES

To learn how to enter obscure characters that can't be found on your keyboard (ALT+Numpad ASCII characters), scan this barcode or go to:

www.LockingTheCookieJar.com/ascii-bk

Most People Use the Same Password for Everything

The single-most powerful fact that helps hackers gain access to a targeted victim's secrets is that most people use the same password for multiple accounts. Even those who should know better still have a false sense of security.

For several years, Mark Zuckerberg, the CEO of Facebook, used "dadada" as his password for his LinkedIn, Pinterest, Instagram, and Twitter accounts. How did the whole world find out about this in June of 2016? It started in 2012 when LinkedIn unknowingly had their database of 6.5 million accounts and passwords stolen. Several years after the theft, the hackers published the list of accounts and passwords on the Internet. Zuckerberg's "dadada" password was in the list along with his LinkedIn account. A hacker correctly guessed that he might use the same password for other accounts and quickly exposed and defaced his Pinterest, Instagram, and Twitter accounts. What if he also used it for his company login or bank account login? The question that begs to be asked is what did the original hackers of the LinkedIn database do with all of those emails and passwords that were likely used for other accounts? Remember, no one even knew they stole the database until 2016!

Studies vary but it appears that 50%-75% of people use the same password for most of their login accounts. If you are one of these people, you should be worried. Why? Because all a hacker has to do is figure out your password for one account and they can access all of your accounts.

The general population doesn't realize that figuring out someone's password can be extremely simple in some systems. Sure, hacking a bank account might be very difficult, but if it uses the same password as a low-security system, you can be at serious risk.

Simply Open the File and Look

It sounds crazy, but sometimes stealing a password is as easy as accessing the database behind the scenes. There are still thousands of computer systems and websites out there that were written by novice developers and have little or no security or encryption built into their design. All a hacker needs to do is open the file containing the logins and passwords and, voila, he has enough personal information to make Sybil's multiple personalities look like child's play.

And while accessing the login database of most online systems is not quite this easy, hackers work hard to figure out how to access it. Once they can access and download the database, they can work on it at their leisure knowing that most people rarely change their passwords.

Unfortunately, some executives at the software development companies and many executives at the purchasing companies have no clue what questions to ask to ensure their software is secure. The LinkedIn login database that was stolen in 2012 and not discovered until 2016 had encrypted passwords, but the hashing algorithm they used (called SHA-1) didn't include a "salting" feature that added random characters into the stored results. This allowed hackers to reverse engineer the database and search for common phrases using the encrypted characters.

There are tens of thousands of horror stories out there. Here are a few:

- LivingSocial got hacked and over 50 million user accounts, emails, names, addresses, dates of birth, and passwords were stolen.
- Federal Reserve internal website was hacked and the personal data of over 4,000 bank executives (names, addresses, phones, email addresses, and fax numbers) was stolen and published online. Ouch.
- eBay.com lost 145 million accounts to hackers.

- JP Morgan Chase, the world's largest bank, had 76 million accounts copied after hackers got access to their highest level of computer administration access.
- Many of the 32 million users who signed up for AshleyMadison.com. an extra-marital affairs website, were revealed to the public, exposing high-ranking executives, government officials, and more.
- Gawker's database of emails and passwords was not only hacked by a group called Gnosis, but they deciphered over 250,000 of the passwords and posted them online! This resulted in millions of accounts on other systems being hacked because people tend to use the same password for multiple accounts. The identify theft damage and financial theft could not be calculated.
- In 2016, Yahoo! discovered that 500 million accounts were stolen... back in 2014! The thieves had two years to use the data undetected!
- Hillary Clinton discovered just how damaging a hack can be after foreign hackers stole and publicly shared her emails. Campaign strategists and Clinton herself feel that she lost a very close

SOURCES

To see hundreds of additional data breaches, scan this barcode or go to:

www.LockingTheCookieJar.com/breaches-bk

presidential election because of the trust concerns by voters over what Russian hackers exposed.

Want to Find Out if You've Been Compromised?

Unless you notice something suspicious or have been notified about a breach, you may never know that your account has been compromised. That is why it is critical that you never use the same password for multiple accounts.

There are some ways that you can find out if your email has been involved in a successful hack. It is nice to know that if you use your email as part of the account ID, you will limit any damage as long as you use unique passwords for each account. In other words, if your Walmart account was hacked, you don't have to worry about your email itself being compromised as long as your passwords are unique. The only time you need to worry about your email being compromised is when it is directly hacked.

In the Sources section below, I've linked to my website that contains several locations that will allow you to enter your email and then find out if it was included in any of the massive data breaches. If it was, then you can change the password and probably be safe at least from that point on.

Remember that just because your email was in a list of hacked accounts, it does not necessarily mean that anyone has specifically hacked your account, figure out your password, or accessed your information. If you haven't noticed a problem, then changing your password should stop any access from that moment forward.

SOURCES

To find out how to detect if you've been compromised (or not) in a data breach, scan this barcode or go to:

www.LockingTheCookieJar.com/detect-bk

There are a few potential clues that should grab your attention if your account has been hacked:

Who Changed My Password?
If your account password is no longer working, it could mean a few things. First, let's assume you tried again and re-typed it more carefully. Second, let's assume your account, whatever it may be, is up to date and was not automatically disabled because of disuse or nonpayment. Third, let's assume you know your password, and you are logging in correctly.

When a password no longer works, it is possible that someone tried to guess the password too many times and locked the account. Not all accounts allow unlimited attempts so if someone was trying to guess the password too many times, it might be locked to secure the account, which means you're safe. Contact the system administrator and find out how to get it reset. There's probably instructions on the login screen to tell you what to do.

Often this requires sending a text to your cell phone, or sending a security key or link to an email, or alternate email if your email account is what is locked.

In the event the system was directly compromised and the hacker got into your system, it can be problematic. If they decided to change your password to keep you out while they have their way with your account, you've got to shut them down right away and then figure out what they might have done. The technique for taking back control of your account depends on what kind of account you have and how it handles lockouts. If there is backup security like secret questions or a text to your cell phone, you can often take back control of the account by following the instructions on their website. Sometimes the system isn't that sophisticated and the hacker might have changed your security questions and alternate email without you getting notified.

Are you sure it was not a friend who thought it would be funny to change your password by accessing your computer when you stepped away? If you believe it truly was a hacker then be prepared to think through what damage he could cause by accessing that account. If it's a major retailer, is it possible he might be purchasing items and paying with your credit card on file? If it's your email, you've gotta accept that he now knows all of the other accounts that use that email. This is where it's critical that you aren't using that same hacked password for any other account!

If you suspect that your credit card or bank account is being used without your permission, check it! Take the time and carefully examine your accounts and ensure you understand every charge.

Footprints in My Email

A smart hacker that obtains access to your email will not change your password because that would be a loud siren that your account was hacked. Then you'd naturally reset the password, and he'd be locked out again.

Although there are ways to hide his tracks, most email hackers are not as careful. The best way to see if he's been in your account is to check your Sent folder, Deleted (or Trash) folder, and your Inbox.

If he sent emails from your account, you may see the remnants in your Sent folder. Is there anything you don't recognize? Can you figure out what he's doing? Did he send spam to your friends? Did he send other emails on your behalf?

If he deleted emails in order to hide his tracks, and forgot to remove those deleted records, you're in luck. Check your Deleted folder. Those deleted emails might be hiding password changes in various accounts, purchases, and other dastardly deeds.

Your Inbox might still contain remnants of what the hacker has been doing. Just like the Deleted folder, look for password changes, receipts for purchases, and other activity.

As mentioned in Chapter 2, your email is a goldmine of information. By examining your emails, a hacker can discover where you bank, which retail accounts you have, which credit cards you own, who your friends are, where you work, your health insurance, and more.

Not from My Computer

When you access email or use certain other software, sometimes the software tracks where you are when you access it. This is usually done by tracking the IP address you are currently at. This IP address is unique between your home, your work, Starbucks, etc. Sometimes it might track via your GPS location, but that is used only in specialized security situations.

Gmail, for example, records the last five IP addresses from which you accessed your Gmail account. To see this list, scroll down to the bottom of your account. If you notice addresses that are not yours, it's a good sign that someone else is using your account. In that case, change your password.

Chapter 4
How to Create a Hacker-proof Password

If you jumped right to this section without reading the sections above, or at least skimming them, congratulations! You figured out that this is one of the most interesting and valuable parts of this book. However, without reading the sections prior to this, you won't thoroughly understand *why* this is so valuable. In contrast, if you have read straight through, the strategy taught in the following sections will make perfect sense and you'll understand why it's such a great technique.

Before I explain how to create a hacker-proof password, let's review what a hacker knows about *most* people. They know that most people:

1. Have a false sense of security
2. Have accounts and passwords written down within three feet of their keyboard
3. Use common, easy-to-guess passwords that are often based on personal information
4. Use short passwords that can be easily determined by a hacking program
5. Use the same password for multiple accounts

Characteristics of a Hacker-proof Password

In order to create a password that cannot be determined by a hacker, it must meet the following characteristics:

- Impossible to guess regardless of how well the hacker knows you
- Complex enough to make discovery mathematically impossible for hacking programs
- Unique for every single account. In case an account is compromised, all other accounts will remain safe

Sounds like a daunting task, right? You're thinking that it will probably be something that creates impossible-to-remember passwords like "Ij83*&%jgwolM@p," right? *Wrong.* What you are about to learn includes two more characteristics that will blow you away!

This will also teach you how to create hacker-proof passwords that are:

- Easy to remember
- And yes...can even be safely written down! In fact, many people do safely write these down or record them in their cell phones

Too good to be true? Nope! Keep reading.

Here are some of the passwords we're talking about. Please understand that when you see the following, it's not what you think. Here are a few examples of these passwords:

- 1$tXB^
- g_eXml
- .fXb!

Let's build the pieces of a hacker-proof password.

Build a Master Phrase

The key to designing a hacker-proof password is determining a master phrase. A master phrase is something that will remain private and will never be written down or recorded in anything that could be easily found or discovered. The only exception to this rule is that you must plan for your spouse, children, or heirs in the event of your death or incapacitation (if you would like someone to be able to access your accounts after your demise).

The master phrase must have these characteristics:

- A phrase that is easily remembered, unique for you, and won't be forgotten
- Between 4 and 8 words long
- Contains upper and lower case initial letters (the first letters of each word)
- Contain numerals
- Does NOT contain special characters other than alpha-numeric characters (because some accounts do not allow special characters)

Here are examples of master phrases. This list includes a few common phrases to give you mind triggers for other ideas. Obviously, these probably won't fit your situation, but they can be good triggers for phrases that would work for you.

- I am John, born in 63
- The War of 1812
- My 2nd child, Della, is my favorite
- Mom died in August 2003
- I proposed to Mary on October 15
- Another 1 bites the dust (song sung by the band, *Queen*)
- I wish they all could be California girls in 65
- Rent 525600 minutes (from the musical, *Rent*)
- There are always 2 sith (from Star Wars)

- Don't know about u but I'm feelin' 22 (Taylor Swift song lyrics)

Convert Your Master Phrase into a Master Key

Use the first characters of each word to create a master key. Be aware that you don't have to stick to this exact rule but you do have to understand how you interpret it. This rule will be tweaked for a few of the phrases so you can see how it benefits.

Taking the previous master phrases, here is what the corresponding master keys could look like:

- "I am John, born in 63" becomes "IaJbi63"
- "The War of 1812" becomes "TWo1812"
- "My 2nd child, Della, is my favorite" becomes "M2cDimf"
- "Mom died in August 2003" becomes "MdiA03" (slightly modified)
- "I proposed to Mary on October 15" becomes "IptMoO15"
- "Another 1 bites the dust" becomes "A1btd"
- "Rent 525600 minutes" becomes "R525600m"
- "There are always 2 sith" becomes "Taa2s"
- "Don't know about u but I'm feelin' 22" becomes "DkaubIf22"

When you create a master key, you need to remember how you did this. Whenever you need to recall your master phrase, it's critical that you can quickly convert it into this exact master key in your mind, every time you do it.

Convert Your Master Key into a Variable

Remember high school algebra where "X" can equal a huge equation?

When X = 4i + 5Y(3Z^4 * A) then anytime you see X, you know it represents the equation. At this point, half of you are freaking out, thinking you need to do some math. No, don't worry. No math required!

Likewise, in simple programming languages, if X = "John Smith" than anytime the variable X is told to display on the screen, the contents of X will display. Hence, John Smith will display.

Assigning your master key to a variable hides the details. This process is the security behind this technique. The cool thing about variables is that you can have a different variable for different types of phrases and this can be super powerful later. As an example, let's assign variables to all of the sample master keys. In reality, you'll probably only use one or two master keys of your choosing so you'll only need one or two variables. You can use X or you can make the variable a little more helpful.

As you'll see later, it's important to be able to pick out the variable when there are other characters around it so after learning the rest of this process, you might want to come back to this step to change the variable name.

People who use more than one variable often try to make the variable mean something that helps remind them what the master phrase is. Let's assign some variables to the master keys from above:

- X = "IaJbi63" ("I am John, born in 63")
- W = "TWo1812" ("The War of 1812")
- <3 = "M2cDimf" ("My 2nd child, Della, is my favorite") NOTE: <3 is a sideways heart for Della.
- MOM = "MdiA03" ("Mom died in August 2003")
- RING = "IptMoO15" ("I proposed to Mary on October 15")

- Q = "A1btd" ("Another 1 bites the dust") NOTE: Q is for Queen, who sang the song.
- R = "R525600m" ("Rent 525600 minutes")
- SW = "Taa2s" ("There are always 2 sith") NOTE: SW is for Star Wars.
- TS = "DkaubIf22" ("Don't know about u but I'm feelin' 22") NOTE: TS is for Taylor Swift, who wrote/sang the song.

As you will discover, making a variable that reminds you of the master phrase will help you quickly decipher your real password later. The key is making sure you use a master phrase that you can easily recite.

www.LockingTheCookieJar.com
92

Create a Pseudo Password Using the Variable

Here's the icing on top of a secure cupcake! Now to complete the creation of a pseudo password, you need to do a little homework about the security system you are dealing with. You can often discover these requirements when you first create your account or if you later try to change the password. Sometimes just viewing your account information shows password minimum requirements.

For example, some password systems allow only alpha-numeric passwords. Some allow any character on the keyboard. Some allow any ASCII character, etc. Figure out what is required and what is allowed. The better systems will say something like, "Passwords must be at least eight characters in length, contain upper and lower case letters, at least two digits, and one special character."

Now all you have to do is take a look at your chosen master key characters and see what else is needed. Therefore, if you have decided to use the "IaJbi63" ("I am John, born in 63") and requirements are that your password must have at least ten characters, both upper and lower case letters, at least one digit, and one special character, then you know you already have most of what's required, and only need at least three more characters to meet the minimum of ten, and a special character.

Now let's add a helpful twist! Let's make the password somewhat self-explanatory so when you write it down, you don't have to also write down what account it belongs to. Therefore, if this will be used for your First Bank account, let's make the variable hint at your account for your quick reference. Because of the sample requirement above, we also need to make sure we have at least 10 characters and a special character.

How about 1$tXB^ (which is really "1$tIaJbi63B^") or 1BX$ ("1BIaJbi63$") or FXB#Wow (FIaJbi63B#Wow)?

So now if you have 1$tXB^ written on a piece of paper or listed in your cell phone, would you remember that it's the password to your First Bank account (thanks to the "1st" and "B^")? Are you starting to smile yet? Prepare to smile bigger because it gets better.

So let's go back to our initial example of passwords. If you saw these written down on a piece of paper or in your cell phone, could you guess what accounts they went to?

- 1$tXB^ (First Bank)
- g_eXml (Google email)
- .fXb! (Facebook)

Good! So let's recap what we just accomplished. We have long passwords that cannot be guessed or calculated via a hacking program. If a bad guy or prying friend saw your list of passwords written down, they would have no idea how to use them. They don't know about your variable X and even if they figured out they were passwords and could guess what accounts they belonged to, they would never enter the right password because they don't know to swap the variable X with the master key "IaJbi63" to know the real passwords!

Now let's look at this from the perspective of a hacker who steals a database containing thousands, even millions, of passwords, including yours. Because you no longer use the same password for every account, they could never access any of your other accounts because the passwords are all different. And remember, if they are viewing your actual password in a database (let's say your Facebook password of ".flaJbi63b!"), they are not seeing the pseudo password of ".fXb!" so they don't even realize that you're using this technique. They don't realize the middle portion of this password is similar to middle portions of other systems. Remember, most hackers are going after easy prey, so when they realize this password won't work for the external accounts they are wanting to target, they usually just move on to the next account in the stolen database.

WARNING ⚠️

Do not write down your master phrase anywhere near your pseudo passwords! Figure out how to inform your spouse or heirs but never write it down where a bad guy can find it. Also, when you do write it down, do not explain what it is in this same location, or else you compromise your security. One idea is to write the master phrase in the family Bible and list the page number in your living will along with an explanation of how to use it. Another idea is to explain how your passwords work and show them where your passwords are written down, but don't tell them what your master phrase or master key is. All they know is that when you die, they can get the variables from your best friend. Give your best friend a piece of paper with the master phrases and ask him to store it in a secure location that he won't forget. Tell him that upon your death, he needs to provide this document to your family. Do not tell your friend how the phrases work.

Mix and Match for Even Better Security

To really boost your security, you'll want to create multiple variables. You can combine variables in the same password or you can use different variables to keep yourself extra safe in the event that one password gets compromised. This works great when you are required by your employer to change your password every so often.

While it's hard to remember several master phrases, most people can remember a few. There are some cool techniques to create variables that are helpful. You might use a variable BIZ to represent the acronym of your favorite business. BB might represent your favorite baseball team. K2 might represent the initials of your 2nd oldest child. HM might represent the street address (numbers) of your home. The ideas can go on and on. Let's list a few examples to explain how they can be combined:

- BIZ = "KP" (Kaiser Permanente)
- biz = "kp" (Kaiser Permanente)
- BB = "OA" (Oakland A's)
- K2 = "MS" (Mary Sue)
- HM = "1234" (1234 Main Street)

This gives you the ability to create passwords that are unlike each other.

For example, let's create pseudo passwords using the variables immediately above and further above:

- Twitter Password = bizTwX (pseudo password) = kpTwIaJbi63 (real password)
- Chase Bank = ChBBXK2 = ChOAIaJbi63MS
- Amazon = XAmzBIZ = IaJbi63AmzKP

Now you should be able to safely write down, or record in your phone, these pseudo passwords: bizTwX, ChBBXK2, and XAmzBIZ. As long as you can recognize that these belong to Twitter, Chase, and Amazon, you can feel confident that these are safe and secure from any thief. Again, it is critical that you do not list your variables anywhere near your passwords because those are the weak link in your safety.

Chapter 5
Identity Theft

"The police can't protect consumers. People need to be more aware and educated about identity theft. You need to be a little bit wiser, a little bit smarter and there's nothing wrong with being skeptical. We live in a time when if you make it easy for someone to steal from you, someone will." – Frank Abagnale

Generally, identity theft is the crime of pretending to be someone else. This might be as simple as using their credit card and buying items on their account. It might be using their healthcare identification information to get free or discounted medical service or medications. It can be as extensive as living a life "as" the victim. This fake life might collect the victim's pension or social security and can own assets such as businesses, stocks, vehicles, land, and houses. Identity thieves can ruin your credit score too.

Protecting yourself from identity theft is not the responsibility of the police or the government or your bank. It's your responsibility. Yes, many institutions who have your private information *might* be obligated to protect it, but it's your duty to regulate how you provide this information and to whom you provide it.

www.LockingTheCookieJar.com
100

Secure Your Social

Remember, your Social Security number (SSN) is your unique identifier. It's theoretically not changeable. Once stolen by the wrong person, you're toast. Even if you get things cleaned up, they can do it all over again or sell it to others to have their turn at your identity.

Safeguard your Social Security card. Do not ever put it in your wallet or purse. Memorize it. Your employer might require a copy of your SSN card as part of the Form I-9, if you don't have a passport, but other than that, it's rare that you'll need the physical card. Lock it in a safe.

Do not write your SSN on your checks and do not use it as an identifier engraved into your assets (a common habit of older generations).

SSN is the Bullseye

The primary target for serious identity theft is your Social Security number. It's not very useful without a full name, address, and birthdate. However, all of these can be obtained very easily. The name, address, and birthdate can often be gathered from a phone book and social media. The Social Security number is the trick.

Your mother's maiden name is also helpful in stealing an identity since it's often a security question. Since these names are not changeable, once it's known, it is a permanent theft. Like many other pieces of information, this can often be figured out through trails in social media, public records, and even ancestry websites. Often the desired information can be determined directly from Facebook profiles and posted information. For example, if your mother's married name is Betty Wilson but she has a brother or father with the last name of Smith, it's probable that her maiden name is Smith.

According to the Identity Theft and Scam Prevention Services website, "With a stolen Social Security number, an identity thief can either assume your identity by using your actual name and biographical information or use your Social Security number in combination with a different name and biographical information in order to create an entirely different identity. This latter form of identity theft involving a social security number combined with a different name is often referred to as synthetic identity theft." [4]

Tax Returns

Identity thieves can use your name and SSN to file your tax return and receive your federal and state refunds. If they file before you do, there is a chance they might be successful, especially if they were careful in how they filed the return. If they file a successful return and get the refund, your return will be rejected since the IRS will think you already received your return.

Many SSN thieves go for a quick score and file fraudulent tax returns designed to bring a nice refund. As mentioned above, they do this early in the new year so they can be sure to file before you do so there's less of a chance of getting rejected. You can help protect yourself by filing early in hopes of beating them in the mail. There isn't much you can do to stop them if they file first, unless it's close enough that the agency hasn't sent out a refund check yet. Otherwise, you'll have to wait until the IRS or your state notifies you that "you" have already filed. They might also surprise you with a request for an audit if the thief gets so wild that it triggers red flags with the agencies.

Working on Your Behalf

Because employees must provide a SSN, illegal aliens and those trying to hide their identity will often provide a stolen SSN or a random SSN which might match yours. Their employer will be reporting earned income under your name that you won't know about.

When you go to file your tax returns, the IRS will think you didn't report all of your earned income and your return might get rejected, you might get audited, and it will be, at the least, a big hassle. In some cases, it could bring fines and penalties your way.

If you think your tax issues are a result of identity theft, you'll have to contact the IRS.

SSN Reboot

It is possible to get assigned a new Social Security number, but trying to notify all the places using the old number can be a serious hassle. You can't just decide to get a new number, either. You have to prove you've had ongoing hassles with identity theft in order to convince the Social Security Administration that you need a new one. So if you had thoughts of changing it to hide that you filed for bankruptcy or some other scheme, tough luck.[5]

Stealing Your Benefits

Stealing your identity also allows the thief to access your benefits *as you*. Not only do they have the chance to use your benefits, but they can change your benefits and cause a world of pain for you and your family.

Borrowing Your Healthcare Benefits

When a thief steals your identity, they can access your healthcare benefits. Not only do they possibly have access to your medical history, but they can get covered medical care under your health plan and use up your covered benefits. This can hurt your credit history by not paying their share (your share) of the deductible.

Victims find it especially frustrating when trying to sort out the medical history down the road. You swear you've only had only two children but your plan shows that you're covering five children on this plan. Your work requires a clear medical history but your doctor won't sign off because of your surprising case of emphysema and COPD that you didn't know you had. And then your spouse got angry when she noticed that your medication history contains Herpes and AIDS-related medications, although you never had either.

Another major problem that can affect victims is when they apply for life insurance. This usually requires a consent to review your medical history. You can end up with much higher medical rates than normal due to health issues your thief has mixed into your history and you can also get denied altogether. Victims often don't take enough time to research the details, especially if they have a few minor health issues. They blindly accept the high rates or move on if they were denied.

Vehicle Insurance Benefits

There have been cases of identity thieves adding additional vehicles to the victim's car insurance plans, and sending the insurance card for the additional vehicles to a different address. Sometimes the thief pays the discounted group rate on a separate bill, thus hiding the trail from the victim. Sometimes the thief adds the additional vehicle to the existing policy and while the insurance card gets mailed to a different address, the victim pays the bill each month.

It's amazing that many victims don't bother to question the sudden increase in rate charges. If you ever suspect that you might be a victim, contact your insurance company and ask for a list of all policies connected to your name.

Life Insurance Benefits
An identify thief can update life insurance benefit plans with additional recipients or replace the existing recipients with completely new ones. To change beneficiaries, the thief often has to make the changes in person but if they've truly stolen your identity, it can be easy to do.

Single, unmarried victims pose a higher risk and the dastardly deed often isn't discovered until the victim is deceased, when it's up to the surviving family to get an attorney and challenge the changes.

Retirement Benefits
If a thief has all of your personal information, they might be able to retire early and collect your benefits. This is a mess to try to straighten out and if they're drawing from a 401k or similar account, it might require a lawyer to recover your losses, if the thief has any assets to lose.

If they have access to your investment account, they can cash out stock, withdraw from your account, and more. If this is what you planned to live on in retirement, you could end up with a significantly lower quality of life at the end of your life.

Unemployment Benefits
Thieves can collect unemployment benefits on your behalf, depleting the funds that could be available for you, should you need it.

Loaning the Coat Off Your Back

Your good credit is often used by thieves to obtain credit cards, buy homes, by vehicles, obtain student loans, personal loans, and even refinance houses. Pretty much any type of loan you can get, a thief with big nads can get. In fact, the thief will probably go after things you might not. After all, it's not his own identity he's hurting and he's not risking his own credit score.

But he is risking jail, so he'll probably be very careful about how he prepares to steal from you. He wants an easy target, which means he needs your information and he needs you to be lazy. I keep saying "he" in this paragraph, but there are a significant number of female identify thieves too. These criminals aren't limited to gender, age, race, or geography.

Applying for a credit card is fairly easy for a criminal if they have your identity. Yes, they use a different address but they can list your current address as their previous address. Once they have a card under your name, they are a shopper with your credit score! They can raise your credit limits and spend away. A smart thief will not spend the card to the max. They will use it responsibly for a while, paying only the minimum payment and letting the card limit max out over time. In the meantime, they'll attempt to obtain as many cards as they can before your credit gets too bad.

Some thieves are able to add child cards to your existing account. Of course, these child cards belong to other stolen identities. When the victim is a real family member, this can be especially cruel.

There have been cases where an identity thief has refinanced the house of a victim, pulled out the equity, and ensuring that the resulting payment is the exact same as it was previously. This hides the crime from the victim until later when the victim attempts to use the equity themselves.

Thieves frequently buy cars, financing them with a low-interest loan under your name. They might pay off the loan in hopes of hiding the credit theft but often they let the bills come to your home and hope the repo company doesn't catch up with them. When that car (*your* car) is involved in a hit-and-run accident or crime, the knock on your front door might include handcuffs.

Don't be the Low Hanging Fruit

Secure that Paper!
We've discussed phishing schemes that trick victims into providing their private information (such as login information and other private data). Aside from simply typing in the information for a bad guy to obtain, providing your information in writing is the worst mistake you can make.

Do you have your tax forms laying on a counter at home when company arrives? Are your bills or receipts easily accessible to a guest? How about a burglar? Do you place your purse next to the front door?

Secure your private records and statements in a locked drawer or cabinet. Thoroughly destroy unnecessary records. A great time for a thief to harvest your information is on garbage pickup night in your neighborhood or via a business dumpster. Even when you leave your office, what are you leaving behind that can be easily stolen or photographed? Were you pre-approved for a new credit card, but just tossed it into the round file? Someone else might appreciate the opportunity to file for that card using your information but their own address.

Before tossing it, destroy credit card statements, bank statements, solicitations, and any other documents that contain private information. That means to tear it up carefully, cross shred it, burn it, or even swallow it if you want high-fiber security.

Don't forget to shred the credit cards too. If your shredder doesn't handle them, cut them carefully to ensure the name, numbers, and code on the back are segmented. Don't throw them away in the same container at the same time.

Do you really need to store 15 credit cards in your wallet or purse? One pickpocket or snatch and run incident can could cause you a significant headache, a headache that could have been avoided. How about removing the unnecessary cards and storing them in your safe when you're not planning to use them? No, don't store them in that kitchen or bedroom drawer! Thieves know about those drawers. How about simply cancelling the cards that do nothing but water down your credit score? Every additional credit card poses a security risk.

AUTHOR SIDEBAR

I'm amazed and shocked how often I'm sitting across the desk from someone who has paperwork and files laying on their desk with confidential information on display. This info is usually their client's, but I've seen personal information on occasion too. I've seen medical records, applications, bank statements, credit card numbers, tax forms, and other documentation. The information listed on these forms contain everything necessary for a dishonest person to steal an identity. When I'm supplying this personal information, I've caught myself asking, "How will you secure my confidential information?" And if I happen to be talking to someone who is accidentally displaying some else's confidential information at their desk, I might add something like, "I'm guessing that Marie Jones would want you to better secure her Social Security number and address." Yes, it might be somewhat savage, but it gets my point across and I'm guessing they'll do a better job with my information, although they might react by purposefully "losing" it in the shredder.

Protect your Mail!

Your mailbox brings you new credit cards, bank statements, credit applications, paychecks, retirement reports, utility bills, and birthday cards with cash.

Outgoing mail contains checks from your personal checkbook, filled-out applications, company checks, confidential forms, and much more. Clearly, mailboxes are a goldmine for thieves.

If you have a traditional mailbox that sits on a wall near your front door or office, or if it is out at the end of your driveway, you may never know if a thief simply opens it and removes your precious contents. To up your security, empty your mailbox quickly or get a P.O. box. When you mail items, place them in the box close to the time the mailman comes by and avoid placing mail in the box the night before pickup. Lifting that red flag not only tells the mailman that you have mail to send, but it tells thieves to come get free gifts.

Place a lock on your slotted mailbox so stealing would require a little more effort than simply opening the mailbox door and reaching in. Remember that random thieves are generally lazy. If your box is harder to get into than your neighbor's, the thief will pass on yours and head next door instead. Maybe your neighbor isn't so awful after all.

When mailing something important, never place it in an unsecured mailbox. Drive to the post office or to a neighborhood with a secured community box. But be aware that more and more criminals are using a pry bar and popping the backs off a community mailbox where they have easy pickings to the mail from your whole street.

Check Your Checks

Yeah, it's the 21st century, but many checks are still cheap quality with little or no security measures. Thieves can digitally scan a check, change the payee information, and reprint on their home inkjet printer using magnetic ink, which can be easily purchased online or at an office supply store. The old-school thieves sometimes use solvents to change the payee. But in reality, even the most advanced checks can be thwarted by simply obtaining the bank account information at the bottom of the check and creating your own checks.

But wait, wouldn't they get caught if they made a check out to themselves? What if they are using a stolen identity to create the bank account in the first place? Then they can make your checks pay the fake account and withdraw the cash.

If a check was stolen, the thief knows the check number and amount. Therefore, changing who the check is written out to can often go undetected. If the check clears, the company or person making the payment assumes it went to the name they originally placed on the check. It would depend on the recipient realizing the payment never came and they'd have to argue with the payor who sees that it cleared. Often people are too lazy to keep digging.

Thieves love lazy people. If you are not religiously verifying all your credit card charges or balancing your checkbook, you will not notice that someone else is using your card or writing an occasional check through your checking account. When most people notice a charge on their statement that they don't recognize, they assume it's legit and ignore it.

Regularly balancing your checkbook and tracking down things that don't make sense goes a long way towards catching improprieties when they occur.

Question Authority

It doesn't work too well as a teenager, but as an adult, it's important that you question authority. Assume you are dealing a scammer whenever you are being asked for personal identification information over the phone or outside of normal service locations such as a bank, realtor's office, or vehicle repair location.

Be defensive with personal information. Many times, it is optional, so when your information is requested, it's reasonable to ask if information such as your SSN or driver's license number is absolutely necessary. Ask about their privacy policy and specifically say that you do not want your information accessible by anyone else. Even if it's required that you provide it to a legitimate company, your concern will often cause the person taking the information to be extra careful with your information.

Over and over again, people all around you fall prey to scams. These scams take advantage of the elderly, the young, and those in specific situations. Here's an example of how a scammer might take advantage of someone, maybe even you.

Let's assume you're selling your home. This situation places two primary pieces of information into the hands of the scammers: your address and the name and contact info of your realtor. From your address, it's easy to obtain your name and phone number.

What if you received a call from a scammer saying something like, "Hi Mr. Jones, this is Mary Altman. I'm working for your realtor, Mark Davis, trying to finish your selling paperwork. I know you've provided some of this information previously but I need to get one final form turned in today to meet our deadline. Can I verify that your street address is 123 Main Street? What is your date of birth? What is your Social Security number? What is your mother's maiden name? And can I please have the location of where you were born?"

As long as you're cooperative, the scammer can easily keep asking questions as long as you keep answering them. They might ask for your employer, your previous addresses, your anniversary date, the name of your spouse and their SSN, names of your children, etc. Understand that at any point in time that the victim finally realizes this is a scam and stops giving information, the scammer still gets to keep the information obtained up to that point, because you can't take back the information you gave. They don't care if they are discovered because they'll call from an unlisted number, burner phone, or untraceable location.

Many people fall for this scam, especially if the scammer stuck to basic questions. Yet, by challenging their authority and quizzing them about details of your sale, you can determine whether they are authentic or not. In the example given above, do not give any answers until you are convinced they are legit. Ask them for their full name and a call back number. Tell them that you will first call your realtor and verify that this information is needed. You can look up the company online and call their main number and ask if that person works there.

Get Off the Lists

Cleanup your life by getting yourself removed from junk mail lists. This may not always work, but you need to start being proactive about selecting the "Unsubscribe" option at the bottom of emails or registering the email as spam in your email system.

The national Do Not Call Registry allows you to add your phone number in order to cut down on unsolicited phone calls. In the United States, this number is (888) 382-1222, but many other countries have similar registries. When a solicitor calls you, do not just hang up on them. Instead, get their attention and tell them that you'd like to have your name permanently removed from their list.

Your bank and credit card accounts often send annual forms that allow you to opt out of solicitations by their affiliate partners. Make sure you don't just toss those forms, but instead fill them out and turn off anything that shares your information with anyone else.

Monitor Your Credit Report

Monitor your own credit report. It's the best way to see if someone is using your identity to get credit cards, loans, and more. There are plenty of free credit reports that you can obtain on an annual basis. Be super careful that you don't merely do a Google search to find one since there are many scamming companies out there also and they'd love for you to fill out their form.

SOURCES

You should check your credit report at least once a year to check for suspicious activity.

To obtain and thoroughly review your credit report, scan this barcode or go to:

www.LockingTheCookieJar.com/credit-bk

If you find something unexpected or suspicious, alert your card company or the creditor immediately. Don't be afraid to be mistaken...it's your privacy and credit that is at stake! Remember, your credit scores are what allow you to buy houses, vehicles, and other expensive items.

Credit protection services can be bought to get a second pair of eyes monitoring your credit. They can alert you any time change takes place with your credit report. Be aware that these services do not guarantee that your identity can't be stolen and they don't guarantee a fix if it is. They only help notify you whenever things affect your credit score. It is your responsibility to be vigilant.

If you don't use department store or bank-issued credit cards, you should seriously consider closing the account. Besides degrading your credit score by having that extra credit available, you leave the door open to another account getting hacked without you knowing about it.

Statements that Make a Statement

You know those bank statements, credit card statements, and department store credit statements that you receive regularly but never bother to review? Yeah, the ones that get mailed to your house in envelopes that never get opened. This includes those who fall under the pressure to "go green" and stop the paper statements but instead receive email statements.

What about 'em? Thieves know that most people do not carefully review their statements. They don't open the envelopes that get tossed in a box or the round file and they certainly stop opening the emails with the promise of, "I'll get to it later." The quickly growing group of autopay people love the cool feature of never having to write and mail in a check, but they don't realize that it enables tremendous laziness since you never really have to look at the statements in order to pay the account.

Those statements will show you when your account is being used by someone else. It might be your unethical family member, your housecleaner, a babysitter, or someone who got your account information from outside sources.

You must faithfully review those statements! Make sure you recognize every single charge, every merchant, every city, and every amount listed! Not only can you discover minor things such as restaurant staff that add generous tips to your bill after you've signed the slip, but you can discover that your Visa card was used in Disneyland to pay for a hotel, theme park tickets, meals, and gift shop purchases while you were at work in Bend, Oregon.

Remember that there are a few smart thieves that are not dumb enough to waste a good account on a Disneyland trip. They know that if they can use the account for smaller purchases, you might never find out. Most people know that their Visa card, for example, often has a balance of a certain amount. Adding a hundred bucks to the monthly bill won't raise flags for most people because they don't check their statements. Of course, adding a

Disneyland trip will certainly get noticed by most folks, and the card will get quickly cancelled, forcing the thief to find another source.

If the thief has access to your online account, they can hide their tracks even better. They can re-direct your statements to get mailed or emailed someplace else so you never even have the choice to see the statement. Then the hacker might change your password and the email attached to the account. Then, several months down the road when you realize you haven't seen a statement in a while and try to login, your password doesn't work. If you're like most people, you might give up at that point. If you click on the "forgot password" option the system sends an email to the hacker's email, not yours. Many systems are modernizing with security features that, for example, send an email to the old email account notifying it that the email is being changed. The notification contains a link that allows the receiver to cancel the change. However, if the hacker has access to your email account, he can delete the incoming notification.

Many systems are also requiring secondary identification such as a hardware ID (bummer if your computer gets stolen), secret question, PIN, or access code sent to your cell phone. When signing up for a credit card, these might be good questions to ask the card company before submitting your application.

Chapter 6
Other Security Techniques

Up to this point, we know how to identify and stop embezzlement. We understand how hackers think and what they are going after. We know to create passwords that are unbreakable, unique, and can even be written down. We can protect ourselves from most identity theft crimes. What other techniques can help us secure our company and our home?

Hardware and Software Deterrents

This is a difficult subject to write about in a book without listing specific hardware and software solutions. But technology changes so frequently that a specific solution might be obsolete or at least somewhat outdated between the time it's written, then published, then sold, then read.

Therefore, we'll instead talk about general solutions and we'll maintain a resource page on our website for more up-to-date specific solutions.

Firewall
A firewall is a security system designed to prevent unauthorized access to or from a private network or computer. Firewalls can be implemented in both hardware and software, or a combination of both.

Network firewalls are used to prevent unauthorized external internet users from accessing private networks or computers connected to the internet, especially intranets. All messages entering or leaving the private network pass through the firewall. The firewall examines every bit of data that passes through and blocks data that does not meet the specified security criteria.

They block hacking attempts and filter out unwanted traffic such as spam, malware, and malicious bots that roam the internet searching for vulnerable systems. Be aware that if a hacker has a legitimate login account and password, the firewall won't know the difference unless logins are restricted to specific MAC addresses (unique identifiers for computer equipment).

Firewalls can be hardware or software but the ideal configuration is a combination of both. Basic hardware firewalls are often found in broadband routers used by home and small business systems. Software firewalls come with Microsoft Windows and Apple iOS but more robust firewalls can be additionally purchased. Software firewalls help protect computers from outside attempts to control or access the computers.

Modern firewalls for network systems tend to be cloud based but hardware firewalls tend to run much faster. They provide plug-and-play setup for a monthly subscription fee. If it's truly in the cloud, you essentially point your internet connections to this gateway service or device so everything runs through it before entering your internal server network or before leaving your network for the outside world.

Because firewalls are the gateway to/from the outside world, they cannot stop internal attacks that take place behind the firewall. If a user downloads a bad file, plugs in an infected thumb drive, or connects an infected laptop, the firewall may be useless.

SOURCES

Because hardware and software deterrent technology can change over time, we moved specific recommendations to an online resource page. To review this technology, scan this barcode or go to:

www.LockingTheCookieJar.com/tech-bk

Keep Operating System and Software Updated

Hackers are forever working to find vulnerabilities in software so they can bypass security and do their evil work. Developers are forever providing patches and software updates to stop the hackers.

These security patches and updates are useless if you don't keep your operating system, drivers, and all installed software updated. Microsoft, Apple, and other leading software providers allow automated updates. Turn the features on! You should consider retiring particularly-susceptible software such as Java or Flash.

It is especially important to keep your security software up to date, including antivirus, anti-malware, anti-spyware, and a firewall software.

Back Up Only What You Want to Keep

What does a hamster and a hard drive have in common? They both live about four years.

"The value of data stored on a computer, often far exceeds the value of the computer! Hardware can be quickly and easily replaced, but data cannot! Companies often insure their computer hardware against theft and loss, but fail to back up their data, which is far more precious!" – T.E. Ronneberg

If you don't back up your data, you will lose it. It's not a question of "if," it's a question of "when."

Back up your data frequently. Many backup systems can be automated. If you back up daily, that means you can only lose a day's worth of data. Back up every hour, it's just an hour of data. Most students know what it's like to type a report and forget to save it along the way, only to lose it when the computer or software glitches.

Back up to a server that is in a different geographical location! If your building burns to the ground and all of your computers and backup computers, you're toast. With new cloud storage systems, it's a sad excuse for any company to not have safe backups of their data.

Test your backups! You don't want to wait until disaster happens to discover that the backups don't work or that you didn't back up everything you need. Where are your software installation codes? What are your accounts? Oh, you saved them in a file on the computer that died? Sad.

Wipe Before Flushing

Discarded tech equipment can be a field day for hackers wanting to exploit you or your company. The target is equipment that contains storage capability such as hard drives, USB flash drives, DVDs, memory cards, and solid-state memory. While many of these storage devices can merely be plugged in to extract the data, motivated hackers can extract data from encrypted and even damaged storage devices.

Deleting files or formatting the hard drive is not enough since the formatting and deletion normally only removes the registry portion of the directory data and not the data itself. Skilled hackers can bypass the directory listing and download the data files. You must use special software or configure your system to overwrite the data with random data when formatting or deleting.

Before you dispose of any storage equipment that might contain sensitive information, wipe and overwrite the data! If you are unable to permanently delete the data, rent a grinder, blow torch, or drop it overboard off a cruise ship.

Default Login

An easy hack can be made to networks, software, and equipment when owners do not change their default login. For example, your home or office WiFi router often has the default password listed on a sticker under the router itself. If your router is physically sitting out in the open, it's easy for someone to look at the sticker for the password. Then they can sit in their car outside your home or office and access your network. If they know what they're doing, they might be able to access data and equipment connected to your network.

If your router has a guest account feature, use it for guests. You don't want a guest accessing your home or office system. Instead, allow the guest account to only have access to the internet and not to your computers, printer, point-of-sale systems, or backup storage system.

It's a good idea to hide the main router from visitors because it's the backbone of your network and many homes and businesses use it for more than just connecting computers to the internet. Security systems (including video storage), phone lines, television, and more may require that router to be operational. If a bad guy damaged, stole, or unplugged it, he might be able to bypass your security system and at least wreak havoc with your network.

Many software packages, network logins, and other accounts have default administrator logins. The admin accounts are the vault door that allows a hacker to obtain access to everything they need to cause you a 4-alarm headache. Often the password is blank or a standard password that anyone with system experience already knows. To keep bad guys out, you must change these passwords to something complex or delete these accounts altogether, depending on the system.

If you ever apply a password or change the password, make sure you carefully record it. This book provides a safe way to write it down but the key point is to remember what it is; otherwise you'll lock yourself out!

A person who is able to obtain access to your network can do a lot of damage to it. He can potentially intercept your network traffic, gain access to sensitive data, upload viruses and malware, and more. It's imperative that you change the default logins and require secure passwords for your router and set a network password for your local WiFi.

Microsoft Windows has made the system more secure by requiring a confirmation or Administrator login information when programs attempt to make changes to certain parts of the system. If you are still using Windows XP, however, be sure to make your default account a non-Admin account. You can still run processes as Administrator from within this account, provided you know the login information. Otherwise, anyone who steps up to your computer after you walk away, can do some serious damage to your computer.

If your system allows you to set the number of login attempts, set it. Without this feature, a hacking program can run forever over the account and mathematically try every combination of numbers and letters for the password until it's successful, unless, of course, you followed the method I proposed in earlier chapters.

If you can set a timeout to automatically log you out of an account, set it. Decide how long you want someone to be able to access an account if someone sits in your seat after you get up and leave.

Secure Connections

The Internet is very convenient and efficient but it's also dangerous. When you buy something from an online store or signup for a newsletter or use social media, you are sharing information about yourself. This information passes through networks which means anyone monitoring a unsecured network can secretly watch the data go buy and collect it. That data could include credit card information, login information, and anything else you can type into a website or send via some email systems.

Beware of open public WiFi. If a hacker can tie into it and setup his monitoring software, he can easily monitor or steal your connection. To help protect your personal information when using online services, make sure you are connected via an encrypted secure connection (SSL/TLS protocol). You can tell when you have this connection in your browser because the web address (URL) will show "https:" instead of "http:" at the beginning. Major email and social media sites require the https connection and it appears that this will become a standard norm over time.

Limit File Uploads

If your website allows file uploads, you need to take special care to ensure you protect your system. Hackers have created some incredibly smart programs that can be disguised as images and other file types. When these are uploaded into your system, they can be nastier than a Trump tweet against Hillary.

If you must allow uploads into your system, store the uploaded files on a separate server or outside of your root directory and only use secured scripts to access them.

Remove Form Autofill

If your web page keeps the auto-fill feature enabled on your website, you're allowing a thief to access the account of people who had their phone, laptop, or tablet stolen. This can not only cause customer satisfaction issues, it can create security vulnerabilities for high-level user accounts, even those with complex passwords.

Security Question Creativity

Many systems are finally starting to require a secondary security question in case your password is compromised. The security questions are designed to ensure it's really you by asking questions that a hacker wouldn't know the answers to. However, we already know that most information about you can be fairly easily discovered through the wonderful world on online search engines, registries, and ancestry websites. What's your mother's maiden name? What was the brand of the first car you drove? What was your second-grade teacher's name? All of this can be researched by a determined hacker.

Come up with creative answers for your security questions. Your first girlfriend might be your mom. Your first car might be a Hot Wheel. Your first address might be the Denver General Hospital or 'crib." Just don't forget your answer.

Don't Forget Your Dumb Smartphones

Smartphones are little computers and they contain a valuable package of data and personal information should it get into the wrong hands. Require that your employees secure the access to the phones. This means fingerprint, passkey, and geometric swipe features where available. If a thief had access to your personal information on that phone including all of the contacts, apps, emails, messages, photos, and log files that are stored on your phone, chances are that he could do a lot of damage.

Make sure you activate the lockout feature and location finder and that you know how to use them if you ever lose your phone. Also make sure your system is making backups in the event of breakage, loss, or theft so you can load the data onto a new phone from the cloud.

PINs

Personal identification numbers (PINs) are commonplace in our society today. Your debit card requires a PIN to use. Newer operating system login schemes require a PIN. Digital home entry keypads, car entry keypads, and many smart phones require PINs. PINs are used for backup security for bank accounts and other valuable access systems.

Easily Hacked

PINs are often easier to guess than passwords. Why? Because the vast majority of PINs are merely easy-to-remember dates or common numbers for the user.

If they're dates, they often start with "19" or "20" so there's only 100 other possibilities (0-99) for the last two digits. But if you think about it, there are probably much less. For example, if it starts with "20" then it's unlikely that it's a future date so if the current year is 2018 then there are only 19 likely possibilities (2000-2018). If it starts with "19" then it's likely on or after their birthdate and if not their birthdate, then it's probably a significant personal date.

People frequently use their birthday, anniversary, child's birthday, graduation years, friend's birthday, death date of an acquaintance, or similar dates. The street number of your home address, business address, previous home addresses, and work address are also common. Then there are famous historical years such as 1776, 1492, 1812, 2000, 1942, 1929. Oh, and don't forget the "current year" as the ultimate lack of creativity.

Some people decide that they don't like thinking too hard or they tire from the exertion required to move their finger to different keys, so they use the same digit repeated (e.g., 2222, 1111). Others use a geometric shape on the keyboard so they type digits in a circle, square, cross, or line.

We all know these dates are probably not very secure, but we use them anyway. We're lazy and we think that a stranger won't know.

Nifty PIN Idea

Almost every phone that has a numeric keypad also has alpha characters for each digit. Since there are only ten digits (0-9) and 26 characters in the English alphabet, each digit has to share multiple alphabetic characters. One (1) and zero (0) are the exception since no letters were assigned to these digits. Digits two through nine, however, each have three or four letters each.

- 2 = A,B,C
- 3 = D,E,F
- 4 = G,H,I
- 5 = J,K,L
- 6 = M,N,O
- 7 = P,Q,R,S
- 8 = T,U,V
- 9 = W,X,Y,Z

Now instead of using an easy-to-guess date, think of a 4-letter word – assuming your PIN is 4 digits long. No, not *that* 4-letter word (3825 = DUCK, right?) since you thought of it so quickly, because it will be too easy to guess. Of course, you would never use your name or something that obvious, but let's assume you decide that you choose the first four letters of your favorite restaurant, Burger King (BURG). When you use the alpha keypad, you discover that this equals 2874. While 2874 isn't an easy number to remember (or guess for hackers), BURG is easy for you to remember. In your cell phone or nearby paper containing written pseudo passwords, you can write "Restaurant" or "BK" as a reminder.

Transposed Digits

Ever wanted to record something like a credit card number, PIN, or safe combination without completely giving it away? There is a simple technique that allows you to scramble some of the numbers to allow for quick deciphering later. This technique can be very simple or very complex, depending on how involved you want the process to be, and how quickly you want to decipher it to get the real number.

Swap Digits

Here's a simple technique. Figure out what your two favorite digits are and swap them. Let's say your favorite single digit is "8" and your second favorite digit is "9." If you swapped these digits in your recorded numbers, you can quickly decipher them in your mind. Let's say the real number is "65829," then the encoded resulting number, using the swap technique, would be "65928." You can write down the encoded number and when it came time to decoding it, you could quickly do it in your head.

Credit Card Considerations

The swap technique works well for people that want to record their credit card number in their cell phone or write it down for quick retrieval for times when your purse or wallet is not easily accessible. It is also helpful when your credit card is stolen. If you had written down the card number and customer service number ahead of time, it would allow you to quickly contact customer service and provide your information.

There are a few considerations you need to think about ahead of time when it comes to writing down a credit card number. First of all, you'll probably want to also record the expiration date (MM/YY) and the security code. You'll need all of these items if you want to make an online purchase with your card and don't have it handy. Because you don't want to write down the complete credit card number, expiration date, and security code so anyone viewing the material can use your credit card, you'll need to be smart about how you do this.

www.LockingTheCookieJar.com

129

The first consideration is the credit card number itself. If you swap two digits, you'll want to be very careful that you don't make it easy to guess which two digits you swapped. A dead giveaway is the digit 4. Why? Because most credit cards are Visa cards and all Visa cards start with the digit 4. If a hacker sees your transposed credit card number that starts with "9346…" they might guess that you decided to swap the digits 4 and 9 because your recorded card number started with 9. They'd correctly guess, in this case, that the real number starts with "4396."

Many people aren't aware of this but Visa always starts with 4, MasterCard starts with 5, American Express starts with 3 (American Express has more digits than other credit cards and they have a 4-digit security code instead of a 3-digit security code), and Discover starts with 6.

One other important point about cards starting with a "3" is that if the second digit is a 3 or 4, it's always an American Express card. If the second digit is a 0, 6, or 8, it's always either a Diner's Club or Carte Blanche card.

Therefore, it's wise to either avoid swapping out the two most widely-used card prefixes, Visa and Master Card (4 and 5), or swapping them with each other as long as you don't list "Visa" or "MC" as a description of the card number. The digits 1, 2, 7, 8, 9, and 0 are the safest to swap.

What about expiration dates? Months' digits start with 0 or 1 (01 through 12), and years are the last two digits of the year so from 2017 through 2029, that first digit after the "20" will always start with 1 or 2. Also realize that the last digit of the year is probably within the next four years so it is very limited as well. Be careful if you're using the transposing technique on the expiration; you'll want to avoid using 1 and 0, and probably 2. This will limit your best transposing numbers down to 7, 8, 9, and maybe 2.

One strategy for encrypting the expiration date so you don't have to limit your transposing numbers down is to use letters for the date. There are many ways to do this but one is to simply reverse the phone pad digits into letters (see Nifty PIN Idea section). It gives you more options since each digit can represent three or four letters, except for one and zero, which can be left alone. For example, the expiration date 05/19 can be changed to 0K1X, removing the "/" to help hide that it's a date. You can then add the encrypted security code to the end of the date so you have a seven or eight-character (if Amex) date plus security code.

TIPS

Speaking of credit cards…let's revisit a comment made earlier in this book just in case you're skipping around.

Have you ever held your credit card while waiting to pay at the store, gas station, or other venue? Do you realize that most smartphones have high-definition cameras and video built in? You wouldn't be the first victim to lose your credit card information because someone in line behind you took a photo or video of you holding the card with the numbers showing in plain sight!

Palm that card, cover the numbers at all times, and do not flip it over in your hand so the security code shows on the back. A few well-timed photos or video clips can be zoomed in later to retrieve the complete numbers! A little caution on your part can keep your bank account from disappearing faster than a pizza at a Weight Watchers convention.

How to Report Possible Cyber Crimes and Stolen Identity

Tax Issues Due to Stolen Identity
If you suspect that you have tax issues because someone is using your identity, the IRS has an identity protection reporting mechanism that you can access via phone or internet:

Phone: 1-800-908-4490

Internet: www.irs.gov/uac/Identity-Protection

You should also file with the sources described below.

Report Identity Theft
The Social Security Administration can't resolve identity theft problems. If you contact them, they will likely refer you to other resources.

If suspect that someone has stolen your identity or misused your Social Security number or other personal information in ways that create credit problems or other problems, you should go to the government's identity theft website, which will guide you through the steps necessary to get a recovery plan established.

Visit www.identitytheft.gov or call 1-877-IDTHEFT (1-877-438-4338).

It's a good one-stop resource managed by the Federal Trade Commission, the nation's consumer protection agency.

Report Cybercrime at the Internet Crime Complaint Center
The Internet Crime Complaint Center (IC3) provides victims of cybercrime with a convenient and easy-to-use reporting mechanism that alerts authorities about suspected criminal or civil violations. Their mission is to receive, develop, and refer criminal complaints regarding the rapidly expanding arena of cybercrime.

After you file a complaint with the IC3, they will send your complaint to the various law enforcement or regulatory agencies that cover the jurisdiction over your situation.

The IC3 serves the broader law enforcement community that combats Internet crime. This includes federal, state, local, and international agencies.

The IC3 is an active partnership between the Federal Bureau of Investigation, the National White Collar Crime Center, and the Bureau of Justice Assistance.

Their website is at www.ic3.gov

1 http://www.brainyquote.com/quotes/keywords/honesty.html#wt7Qr4ykokdM4VBs.99

2 http://www.russmanlaw.com/blog/criminal-defense/embezzlement/how-common-is-embezzlement

3 http://nypost.com/2016/01/19/the-25-most-stolen-passwords-of-2015

4 http://www.identitytheft.info/ssn.aspx

5 https://www.ssa.gov/pubs/EN-05-10064.pdf

www.ingramcontent.com/pod-product-compliance
Lightning Source LLC
Chambersburg PA
CBHW071232020426
42333CB00015B/1431